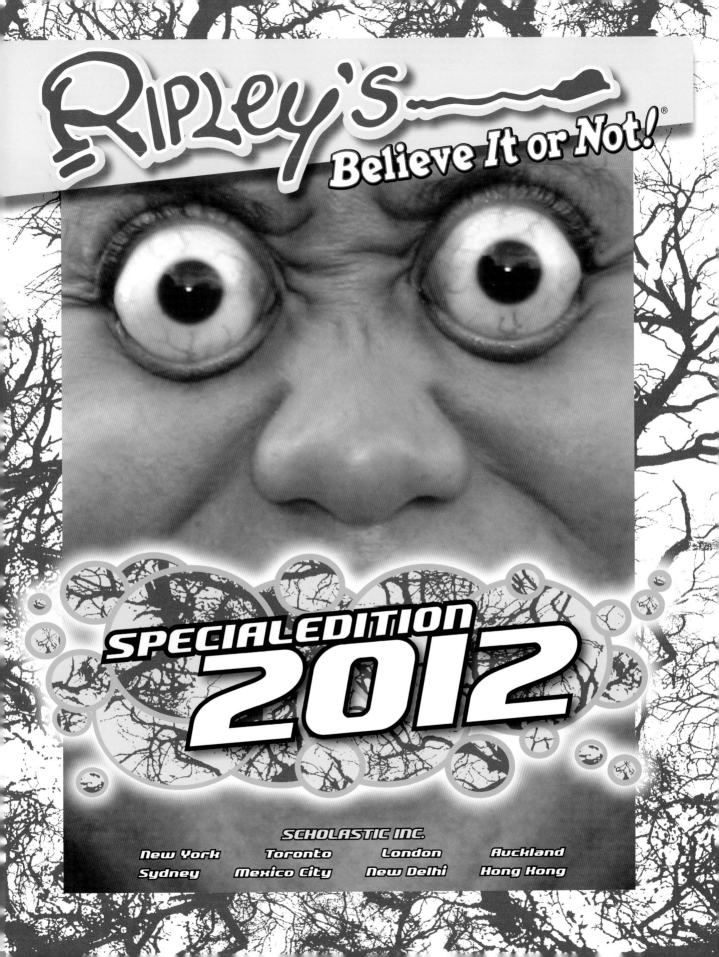

# Ripley's ® Believe It or Not!

## SPECIAL EDITION 2012

SCHOLASTIC INC.

New York    Toronto    London    Auckland
Sydney    Mexico City    New Delhi    Hong Kong

ISBN 978-0-545-32975-0

**PUBLISHING**

Developed and produced by Ripley Publishing Ltd

Publisher: Anne Marshall
Editorial Director: Becky Miles
Art Director: Sam South

Project Editor: Rosie Alexander
Assistant Editor: Charlotte Howell
Senior Researcher: James Proud
Design: Rocket Design (East Anglia) Ltd
Indexer: Hilary Bird
Reprographics: Juice Creative

12 11 10 9 8 7 6 5 4 3 2 1          11 12 13 14 15 16/0

Printed in China                              82
Lenticular printed in New Zealand
First printing, September 2011

p98

p106

p127

# CONTENTS

p138

p115

p34

# REVEALING...
# THE RIPLEY WORLD

Sweep a flashlight over the darkened storage warehouse at Ripley's HQ in Florida, and the nighttime activity depicted in the Hollywood blockbuster *Night at the Museum* may suddenly seem not so strange. Imagine, as night falls, Ripley's artifacts twisting through the sawdust, sitting up in their crates, easing off their stiffness, and coming to life. A 7-foot, 9,400-pound rubber band ball could start rolling around, a twin-headed calf might shuffle by, tallest man Robert Wadlow's wax replica would tower over your head, and don't even think about what the 37-inch-round hairball found in a cow's stomach might do!

The world of Ripley's is a vast, complicated machine. There are researchers, curators, archivists (juggling 25,000 artifacts, 25,000 photos, and 100,000 cartoons), model-makers, haulage experts, and forklift truck operators moving boxes and displays, as well as editors and correspondents—all making it their business to uncover and preserve the oddities in life.

It was in 1918 that Robert Ripley began his quest to expose the world's most unbelievable true stories. He was working as a cartoonist on the *New York Globe,* and although he initially focused on highlighting "Believe It or Not" achievements in athletics alone, he soon broadened his search to include the whole of humanity all around the world. Ripley traveled constantly, collecting material everywhere he went. He covered over 464,000 miles in his lifetime, and his readership responded to his enthusiasm by posting him up to 170,000 letters every week, each one containing a peculiar tale.

A cleaning-mop ram by artist Federico Uribe.

**La BASTILLE**
—Famous French Prison

IT WAS A MOST LUXURIOUS PLACE!
IT WAS A GAY PLACE—MORE LIKE A CLUB
THAN A PRISON—WHERE EVERYONE
LIVED AS ONE PLEASED—WINE
WOMEN AND SONG, ETC.—PRISONERS
WERE LOATHE TO LEAVE

BEARD
8 FT. LONG
Grown by
EDWIN SMITH
Adrian, Mich.
in 16 years

Signature of
GLENN GORDON
an ARTIST in DALLAS, Texas

A. HERRING
IS A
FISH BUYER
in ILLINOIS, Iowa

SAME
SOX
WORN 22 YEARS
by GUY A. DEAN
Folkston, Ga.

J. W. JOHNSON—Hendersonville, N.C.
GRADUATED from COLLEGE at the AGE of 76!

"I have been called a liar more than anybody in the world.
I feel flattered. That short and ugly word is like music
to my ears. I am complimented, because it means that my
paragraph that day contained some strange fact that was
unbelievable—and therefore most interesting, and that the
reader did not know the truth when he saw it..."

Robert Ripley

A sculpture of a dog made from discarded toys.

By the time he died in 1949, Ripley was a
celebrity and thousands lined the streets of
New York to watch his coffin pass by.
Today, every year, 12 million visitors
pass through the turnstiles of the
31 museums in 11 countries.
Countless more keep in touch
via the Ripley's TV and radio
shows, the BION cartoon—
which is available worldwide—
books, posters, websites, games,
and cell phone downloads. Ripley's
is a big machine that depends on people
worldwide for its amazing material. So keep in
touch, stay on board, and come along for the ride.

# Step inside...

Flick on a news channel and you'll hear all about major sports events, natural disasters, and politics, but have you ever wondered what the rest of the planet's up to? If that's a yes, you should start your investigation right here. Our world is brim full of truly extraordinary people who try out the far side of life. It's bustling and busy with curious critters, fabulous facts, incredible inventions, and magical miracles, to name just a few. And Ripley's salutes them all!

## ZOOM IN!

Identify the close-up and follow the clues to discover a new story.

PAGE 24

PAGE 120

## SAY WHAT!

Keep an eye out throughout the book for these little hits of information that pack a big punch.

PAGE 112

The black and white pictures on pages 42-43 and 88-89 are taken from the Ripley Archive, a vast photographic source that collects together Robert Ripley's own photographs and those sent in to him over the years. The images often formed the basis for Ripley's cartoons in the *New York Globe*. The BION cartoons are still produced today on a daily basis.

PAGE 89

PAGE 49

Every inch of this *Special Edition* is packed with wonderful weird-ities and phenomenal pictures to pore over. Gasp and grimace as you find the men who like to jump bulls, the Mickey-Mouse-patterned puppy, a blood-powered lamp, the boy saved from certain death by the size of his ears, or a succulent, rodent-flavored meal. Each story is an inspiration, part of a celebration of the diversity of life. Turn the page and let the eye-popping begin.

*"This old world is a mighty interesting place."*
ROBERT RIPLEY

WISH YOU WERE HERE

# PLANET EARTH

## Cry Me a River

Austfonna, the second largest ice cap in Europe, is losing about 1.6 cubic miles of ice a year. This image reveals a mournful face sculpted by the melting ice, crying a river of tears. Some people have suggested that the face represents Mother Nature weeping over the effects of global warming, while others think it looks like the late Michael Jackson.

## Dazzling Discovery

In a silver mine deep below the Mexican desert lies a cavern containing crystals over 35 feet long and weighing up to 55 tons each. Warmed by molten rock in the Earth's crust, the crystal cave is a place of extremes— the temperature is over 120°F and the humidity is almost 100 percent. Some of the selenite crystals contain pollen that was trapped 30,000 years ago.

# Don't Look Down

Perched at the top of Africa's Victoria Falls—a thundering curtain of water on the border between Zambia and Zimbabwe—the Devil's Swimming Pool could be the most hair-raising infinity pool in the world. Thrill-seeking swimmers jump in and are swept toward the precipice at frightening speed by the raging torrent. Just inches from the 360-foot drop, a lip of rock saves them from being washed to their deaths.

ARCHH!

## Fall Guys

If you think swimming to the edge of a thundering waterfall doesn't have quite enough buzz, think of these daredevils who went the whole hog and plunged over the 180-foot-high Horseshoe Falls of Niagara, in Canada.

In 1901, Annie Edison Taylor dropped down in a barrel, emerging with a small scratch on her forehead.

William Red Hill Sr. went over in 1930 in a barrel with air holes plugged with corks. At the bottom he was trapped in a whirlpool for three hours but finally emerged alive.

In 1961, Nathan Boya survived the drop, using a steel sphere wrapped in rubber.

Survivors Peter DeBernardi and Jeffrey Petkovich wore hockey helmets inside their 10-x-5-foot barrel, in 1989.

In 1995, Robert Overacker raced over the edge on a Jet Ski, but died when his rocket-propelled parachute failed to open.

Kirk Jones took on the Falls in 2003 without any protection whatsoever, received a fine of $2,300, and was banned from Canada for life.

## SAY WHAT!

Scientists have made diamonds from peanut butter by squeezing it between the tips of two diamonds at a pressure higher than that found at the center of the Earth.

11

# ON THE ROCKS

## SAY WHAT!

Although Mount Everest is the world's highest mountain when measured from sea level, the peak of Ecuador's Mount Chimborazo is actually farther from the center of the Earth because the planet bulges out at the equator.

## Balancing Act

San Francisco artist Bill Dan has been balancing rocks, pebbles, and boulders on one another since 1994. It takes a very steady hand to create these gravity-defying sculptures, but just one strong gust of wind can reduce them to nothing more than a pile of rocks.

## Catastrophic Crater

Tropical storm Agatha caused widespread flooding in Guatemala City in 2010 and it is thought that a sewer leak eroded the city's loose volcanic soil, causing the ground above it to collapse. The 66-foot-wide, 100-foot-deep sinkhole that was created swallowed up a three-story building, killing at least one man.

# Global Village

The company that built the Palm Jumeirah island off the coast of Dubai has an even more ambitious project under construction. The World is a group of 250 to 300 artificial islands in the shape of a map of the Earth. The foundations were created from 11 billion cubic feet of sand and over 50 million tons of rock.

# Perilous Pose

Brave boulder balancers with a head for heights line up to take advantage of this dramatic photo opportunity on top of the Kjeragbolten. The six-foot-wide lump of granite is wedged in a crevasse in the Kjerag mountain, Norway, 3,300 feet above the icy waters of the fjord below.

# BIG BRIGHT WORLD

## Brilliant Blooms

Professor Chia Tet Fatt from Singapore has created a nightlight by combining DNA from a firefly and tissues from orchids to create glow-in-the-dark plants. The roots, stems, leaves, and petals of the genetically modified orchids create their own greenish-white light for up to five hours at a time.

## Snowy Seas

Seafarers often tell tales of glowing, milky seas that resemble a surreal snowfield stretching to the horizon. Now satellite pictures have confirmed mariners' reports that an area of the Indian Ocean, the size of Connecticut, was glowing for three nights in a row. Scientists believe that the phenomenon is caused by luminous bacteria.

# Kaleidoscopic Colors

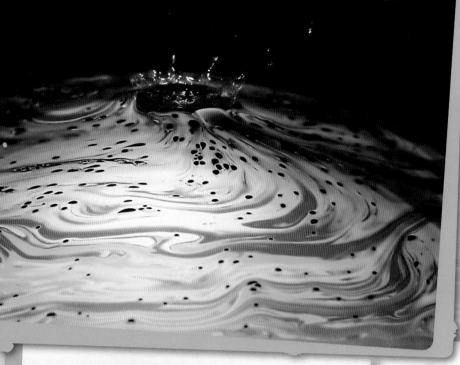

The colors that appear just before a bubble bursts are produced when light waves are reflected from both the outside and inside surfaces and the waves get out of step. The colors depend on the thickness of the soap film—the thinnest areas look black and the thickest appear red.

# Red Flag Beach

Each fall, the beach in Panjin, northeast China, turns fiery red thanks to a little plant called the sea-blite, which grows on the mudflats. In 2009, local soldiers positioned five stars among the scarlet foliage to recreate the Chinese national flag in celebration of the 60th anniversary of the People's Republic.

## SAY WHAT!

Residents of Omsk, Siberia, were mystified in 2007 when orange snow started to fall. The snow may have been colored by a sandstorm in neighboring Kazakhstan.

# JOURNEY TIME

## Underground Art

Lucy Sparrow has recreated the London Underground map on white felt using 2,625 yards of thread and 142 buttons. The British textile artist carefully embroidered the names of all 270 stations, and she plans to make felt maps of other subway systems in the future.

## Cause for Reflection

The mirror-image Topsy-Turvy Bus was built by car artist Tom Kennedy and his ten-man crew, who welded two school buses together to make the point that government spending is upside down. The project was the idea of Ben Cohen of Ben & Jerry's ice-cream fame, who wanted to urge presidential candidates to spend more money on education and less on the military.

# The Gods' Guest House

Guests of the Tianzi (meaning Son of Heaven) Hotel in China should enjoy their stay as the ten-story building is built in the form of Shou, Fu, and Lu, the gods of Longevity, Fortune, and Happiness. The entrance is close to Shou's foot and the peach in his hand is the hotel's presidential suite.

# Just Slot Inn

You could have trouble finding your key card if you put it down in Manhattan's Key Card Hotel. Built by expert card-stacker Bryan Berg, everything in this fully furnished bedroom, bathroom, and hotel lobby has been made from the plastic cards. It took four months and 200,000 cards to complete the 400-square-foot construction.

# STREETS AHEAD

## Grand Illusion

Those who dream of impressing the neighbors by replacing the rust bucket in their garage with a racing car should contact German artist Thomas Sassenbach. His company, Style-Your-Garage, sells convincing 3-D murals that can be attached to drab garage doors. Images include landscapes, classic cars, and animals—so you could even have a baby elephant in your garage.

## Compact Cottage

Built in 1912, the front of this pint-sized property in Toronto is just over seven feet wide. The owners have made the most of the 300-square-foot space. The baby bungalow has a living room, a bedroom with a wall bed, a bathroom, and a kitchen complete with laundry center. It even boasts a storage basement and a tiny garden.

# It's a Wrap

An insurance company blanketed Britain's most accident-prone street with 1,800 square yards of bubble wrap to highlight the need for careful driving in icy weather. Eight men spent 12 hours wrapping everything in the street—nicknamed Accident Avenue—from houses and sidewalks to trash cans and garden gnomes.

# Parking Fine

Corrine Vau and friends turned an ordinary parking space in Paris, France, into a fun-filled picnic area to celebrate World Parking Day in 2010. This is an annual event when artists, activists, and citizens from around the world temporarily transform parking spaces into fun social spaces.

# WALK OF LIFE

British adventurer Ed Stafford set out to walk the length of the Amazon in April 2008. An incredible 6,000 miles and 859 days later, the former army captain completed his epic journey, during which he contracted a disfiguring skin disease, was stung by wasps, bees, scorpions, and bullet ants, and suffered an estimated 50,000 mosquito bites. He was accompanied by Peruvian forestry worker "Cho" Rivera after his original partner returned home.

## "Just Asking"

**What was the most difficult thing to cope with on the trip?** Boredom. I love the jungle and used to thrive off the adventure of walking through the trees, never knowing what you are going to come across. But, after about two years, both Cho and I got bored. The scary stuff, such as hostile tribes and big snakes, was easy to deal with, as it was dangerous and fun. When things went smoothly, that's when we found it hard to stay positive.

**Six weeks after finishing, what sort of condition are you in?** I'm still not in good shape. My spine is out of line and my legs are tight and full of scar tissue. I'm having regular acupuncture.

**What were you most pleased to see and have when you got back?** We lived off piranhas so I longed for fish and chips with mushy peas, wrapped in paper and eaten on a cold park bench before they go soggy.

# IN ALL WEATHERS

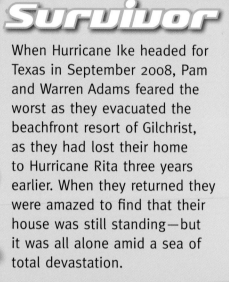

## Sole Survivor

When Hurricane Ike headed for Texas in September 2008, Pam and Warren Adams feared the worst as they evacuated the beachfront resort of Gilchrist, as they had lost their home to Hurricane Rita three years earlier. When they returned they were amazed to find that their house was still standing—but it was all alone amid a sea of total devastation.

## Snap Happy

Lucky photographer Rochelle Coffey captured the image of a lifetime when she caught on camera the rare moment when a river ran red. The place? Cameron Creek in the Canadian Rockies. Heavy rainfall earlier in the day had washed the red sediment argolite from the rocks and Rochelle snapped as it turned the water the color of delicious tomato soup.

RUNNN...

# Desert Storm

Day suddenly turned to night in Golmud, northwest China, when a sandstorm raced into town at 70 feet per minute. The storm, which struck in May 2010, left the 200,000 residents with a major cleanup operation as the mile-high cloud of dust settled. Golmud lies close to the Gobi Desert, which is expanding each year. There are plans to plant a 2,800-mile ring of forest, called the Green Wall of China, around its borders to try to contain it.

# FOREIGN FOOD

## Mouse Drop Soup

A woman was horrified to find a whole mouse in the hot pot she was sharing with friends at a fish restaurant in Jingmen, China. She picked up the mouse with her chopsticks thinking it was a chunk of fish. Inspectors found that the mouse was not fully cooked, so it probably fell into the stew after it had been prepared.

## Shell Shock

English farmer Jeff Taylor got a surprise when he cracked open his boiled egg to find a smaller egg, complete with shell, inside. This rare phenomenon is estimated to occur only once in every three million eggs. It happens when an egg gets pushed back up the bird's oviduct and a second egg forms inside the first.

**SAY WHAT!**

To us they are cute, furry pets, but in Peru guinea pigs are lunch. Peruvians eat about 65 million of the rodents each year.

24

# It's a Whopper

Christy Harp should be able to light up the whole street with a jack-o'-lantern made from this 1,725-pound monster, which took first prize at the Ohio Valley Giant Pumpkin Growers weigh-off. The math teacher said that the pumpkin was putting on 33 pounds a day at one point. Her recipe for success is lots of compost, coffee grounds, and cow manure.

CREAK

# Freaky Food Stuffs

Sushi has become a regular part of our menus, so how long before we get a taste for other foreign specialties? In Indonesia, bat meat is considered delicious and good for respiratory problems, while Mexicans enjoy the eggs of the giant black liometopum ant. In China and Korea rice wine infused with baby mice is a tonic and in Sardinia cheese crawling with maggots is a delicacy.

**OUT OF THIS WORLD**

## Wild Wind

In 1996, a weather station on Barrow Island, off the coast of Western Australia, registered a wind gust of 254 mph during tropical cyclone Olivia. According to the Beaufort scale, the average speed of a hurricane-force wind is 73 mph.

## Tilted Tower

The 35-story Capital Gate skyscraper in Abu Dhabi, the capital of the United Arab Emirates, has been designed with a dramatic 18-degree tilt to the west—more than four times that of the famous Leaning Tower of Pisa in Italy, which has a four-degree incline.

## Landed Gentry

Just 0.6 percent of the population of Great Britain currently owns 69 percent of the island's land. Much of the land has belonged to the same families since the 19th century.

## Silent Speakers

American Sign Language, the first language of many deaf North Americans, is thought to be the fourth most commonly used language in the U.S.A.

## Odd Population

Only about 15 percent of the 1.8 million people living in Dubai in the United Arab Emirates are natives of the country, and men outnumber women by three to one.

## Hidden Peaks

The Gamburtsev Mountains in Antarctica are thought to be about the size of the European Alps but they were only discovered in 1958 because they are completely covered by more than 2,000 feet of ice and snow.

## Lonely Land

Nunavut, the largest Canadian territory, is about the size of Western Europe but has a population of just 30,000. That's fewer than the number of people living in the Mediterranean principality of Monaco, which is a million times smaller.

## Space Junk

When the space station Skylab broke up over the Indian Ocean in 1979, debris landed on the town of Esperance in Western Australia. The town council issued the U.S.A. a ticket for littering, but the fine of $400 went unpaid until April 2009, when California-based radio broadcaster Scott Barley raised the funds from his morning show's listeners and sent the money on behalf of NASA.

## Harmful Habit

The Indians chew paan like we chew gum. The mixture of nuts, spices, and lime paste wrapped in a betel leaf is believed to aid digestion, but pedestrians' habit of spitting out the acidic, chewed paan is corroding Kolkata's Howrah Bridge. The landmark steel bridge has lost 50 percent of its strength over the past three years.

## Give a Little Whistle

Back in Roman times, inhabitants of La Gomera in the Canary Islands developed a whistling language called Silbo so they could communicate across the volcanic island's deep ravines. Silbo still survives today and is now taught to local children as part of the school curriculum.

## Lake in Lake

Lake Manitou on Manitoulin Island, Canada, is the largest "lake in a lake," as the island lies within Lake Huron. Lake Manitou also has two islands, making them islands in a lake on an island in another lake.

## Dear Dollhouse

The figure $169,000 might sound pricey for a dollhouse, but not when it comes with a real house thrown in. Gerry and Cindy Mann came up with this creative buy-one-get-one-free idea when they found it difficult to sell their home in Battle Creek, Michigan. Cindy's father originally made the one-foot-to-one-inch replica of their house for their children to enjoy.

## Semiprecious Sand

Papakolea Beach in Hawaii has olive-green sand thanks to the presence of a semiprecious stone named, appropriately, olivine.

# SEND A POSTCARD

ZOOM IN!

If you think that creating a portrait in stamps is a massive undertaking, consider the tasty artwork on page 117.

## Pooch Post

The unique polar dog mail service serves one of the world's most unusual hotels. The Noorderlicht, aka the "Ship in the Ice" hotel, is a 100-year-old schooner that normally sails the Arctic waters, but in winter it becomes a hotel, frozen in the polar ice. The canine couriers carry guests' letters to the nearest post office 40 miles away.

## Post-Modern Portrait

Portraits of famous people often appear on postage stamps but British artist Peter Mason creates pictures of well-known faces with stamps. A large portrait takes up to 20,000 used stamps, each of which has to be soaked to remove it from the envelope, then dried and sorted. As well as Winston Churchill, his subjects have included Barack Obama, Nelson Mandela, and Princess Diana.

# Green Greetings

This greeting card from China could be a real pet-pleaser. Perfect for a bunny's birthday, the base of the card contains grass seed and nutrients. Just add water and it will grow into a lush little lawn.

# World's Smallest Post Service

Lea Redmond, postmistress of the WSPS, sets up her miniature roll-top desk in cafés around San Francisco and copies customers' messages onto notepaper barely bigger than a postage stamp. The tiny transcriptions are folded into mini envelopes and sealed with wax melted by the flame of a birthday candle. Each nano-note comes with its own tiny magnifying glass.

NOTHING VENTURED NOTHING GAINED

# HIGHS & LOWS

## Don't Drop Off

When it's time for mountain climbers to bed down for the night they might look for a handy ledge—or they could take the ledge with them. The Portaledge is like a small platform that can be suspended from the rock face. Restless sleepers are advised to keep their harnesses attached.

## Flying Leap

Extreme sports star Valery Rozov spent two days climbing 15,100 feet up Mount Elbrus, in the Caucasus mountain range, before taking a one-minute leap from one of the mountain's peaks wearing a wingsuit. The following year, the Russian BASE jumper skydived from a helicopter into the active Mutnovsky volcano. After dropping below the rim of the crater, he opened his parachute and landed on ice in the middle.

# Splash Down

With more than 25 years of professional high-diving experience you would not expect Darren Taylor, a.k.a. Professor Splash, to bellyflop into the water, but Darren dives from a height of 35 feet into a pool just 12 inches deep. He makes a massive splash as he bounces horizontally across the water to slow his body down.

# Not for the Faint-Hearted

The lake of Weissensee in Austria has hosted the first-ever underwater ice-hockey world championship. Eight international teams competed in water that was just above freezing. Players swam upside down, chasing a floating puck across the underside of the 12-inch-thick ice, and had to surface for air every 30 seconds through carefully placed ice holes (right).

# DARE YOU?

## In Hot Water

C.J. Kanuha couldn't afford to wipe out when he went surfing close to the molten lava of Hawaii's Kilauea volcano. The lava had heated the water to over 400°F in some spots, which melted the wax on his surfboard and made the skin on his legs peel. The professional surfer left an offering for Pele, the Hawaiian goddess of fire, before his risky stunt.

## Without a Paddle

Is it a boat? Is it a plane? Daredevil base jumper Miles Daisher has combined skydiving and kayaking to create the sport of "skyaking." Daisher jumps from altitudes of up to 13,000 feet and falls at about 100 mph before opening his parachute and making a smooth landing on the water below.

# Extreme Boating

Its turquoise waters look inviting, but the crater of the Ijen volcano in Indonesia is home to the world's largest lake of sulfuric acid. Canadian adventurer George Kourounis chose to explore this deadly environment by taking a boat into its center.

## "Just Asking"

**George, what runs through your mind when you are floating in a flimsy boat on a deadly lake, potentially being showered by acid droplets?** "What have I gotten myself into this time?" While I was in the middle of the lake, taking pH measurements, some acid got into the boat and started to burn my legs. I had to quickly paddle back and use a knife to cut off my pant legs. Sinking, or falling overboard was not an option.

**Describe the surrounding atmosphere.** Sulfur dioxide gas comes billowing out from volcanic fumaroles and when that gas cloud hits you, your lungs sting and your eyes water. The gas combines with moisture in your body to create sulfuric acid. The smell is overpowering and the whole place feels like you're visiting a hostile alien planet.

**What effect did the acid have on the boat you were in?** The boat itself was made of rubber, so I knew that it should've been resistant to the acid, but I didn't know if the seams that hold the rubber pieces together were going to hold. The paddles I was using were metal and they started to corrode very quickly. I had rubber gloves and a gas mask with me to help protect myself from the acid, but even with all this, I was only able to stay out on the lake for about 20 minutes.

**Why do you do it?** My self-proclaimed purpose in life is to explore the most extreme places on Earth and then share what I've seen with as many people as possible. There are so many odd places that most people don't even know exist.

# YOU MUST BE JOKING

## Hard to Crack

Joe Alexander from Hamburg, Germany, broke a stack of 11 concrete blocks with his elbow while holding a raw egg in his hand. The egg survived because eggs are tougher than they look. If you put one in your palm and wrap your fingers around it, you can squeeze it quite hard without breaking it, as long as the pressure is evenly spread.

**ZOOM IN!**

It's great to get up close with the big cats at a safari park, but the couple in the car on pages 132–133 got closer than they expected.

**COOCHY COO**

## That Tickles

Few people would want to get this close to a 560-pound lion but British wildlife expert Alex Larenty has known Jamu for six years and feels quite safe around him and his pride. Jamu lives at the Lion Park, near Johannesburg, South Africa, and loves getting massages and foot rubs from the skilled animal handler.

# How Do You Do

Steve England was amazed when a wild squirrel came up to him in the woods and took a hazelnut from his hand. The British bushcraft expert had been taking photographs when the squirrel approached him. It moved closer when he took out the nut and finally built up the courage to take it.

## SAY WHAT!

Two escapees from an Argentinian jail evaded capture by disguising themselves as sheep. The convicts wore sheepskins, complete with heads, and hid among a large flock. The 300 policemen on their trail found it impossible to spot the pair among the thousands of sheep that roam the area.

# Back to Nature

Centuries ago, people had nosegays of flowers to cover up unpleasant smells. Now city dwellers can bring the natural world to the busy streets with Bio-Accessories. Made by Melbourne designers Ben Landau and Brittany Veitch, they are meant to mask the sights, sounds, and smells of the city—but wearers should still keep an eye open for traffic!

# LEAPS OF FAITH

Each year, teams of five to seven "recortadores," or bull-leapers, gather in Valencia, Spain, to compete in a dangerous game of chance. Facing up to three bulls in the ring at a time, the teams of bull-leapers fly through the air with amazing skill and agility as the bulls charge toward them. Their acrobatic performances can last for four to five hours and the bulls are not harmed during the daring display.

# Long Game

Bull-leaping dates back to the Bronze Age. It was an important ritual for the late-Minoan people, who lived on the Greek island of Crete between the 17th and 15th centuries BC, and is illustrated in wall paintings from the Minoan Palace of Knossos that still exist today.

# KEEP GOING

## Zoo Quest

Marla Taviano dreamed of seeing the world's wildlife with her family but they needed to do it on a budget, so she came up with the idea of visiting 52 zoos in 52 weeks. Marla, her husband, and their three daughters started their 22,000-mile tour at Louisville Zoo, Kentucky, and ended it in Ohio at their hometown Columbus Zoo and Aquarium.

**BRRRR**

### SAY WHAT!

British TV presenter Helen Skelton encountered caimans, anacondas, and piranhas during her 2,010-mile solo kayak trip down the Amazon River. She made more than a million strokes, paddling about 60 miles a day, six days a week for six weeks.

## Global Triathlon

Extreme athlete Dan Martin is training for an 18-month triathlon that will circumnavigate the Earth. Starting in Nova Scotia, Canada, the British teacher will swim 3,600 miles across the shark-infested waters of the Atlantic to Brest, France, then cycle through Europe and cross the Bering Straits to Alaska. He will complete his epic journey by running across Canada, back to his starting point.

# Solo Sailor

Australian schoolgirl Jessica Watson battled massive waves in her 34-foot yacht, *Ella's Pink Lady*, to achieve her childhood dream of sailing solo around the world. The 16-year-old, who spent 210 days at sea and traveled 23,000 nautical miles, was given the pink carpet treatment on her return to Sydney in May 2010, where she was presented with the gift of a free driving lesson by prime minister Kevin Rudd.

Jessica Watson

# High Ambitions

Jordan Romero from California has a necklace made from rock taken from the top of Mount Everest—that he collected himself! Age 13, Jordan became the youngest person to reach the summit of Everest as part of his quest to conquer the highest peaks on each of the seven continents. He has already scaled Kilimanjaro, Mount Elbrus, Aconcagua, Mount McKinley, and Mount Kosciuszko, and is looking forward to tackling the Vinson Massif in Antarctica.

# OPEN THE ALBUM

OK!

## PRESCHOOLER POWER

This little boy's dad must have thought twice before ticking him off—the four-year-old can be seen here lifting a fully grown man on his shoulders.

EASY!

## BENDY BODY

There must be easier ways to see what's behind you than by striking this painful-looking pose, as demonstrated by a contortionist in the 1940s.

## HUMAN FLAG

The human flag is a popular free-running move but, as this photograph from 1946 shows, the stunt is not new. Lawrence J. Frankel is pictured here holding his body horizontally with 100-pound weights attached to his back.

## SUPER SCRIBE

Zelma George of Canton, Ohio, pictured here in 1948, could write forward, backward, upside down, and upside down backward, as well as writing different sentences in any direction, using both hands simultaneously.

## BALL BALANCER

Julius B. Schuster from Jeannette, Pennsylvania, was able to pick up ten pool balls at once from a flat surface and could balance 20 pool balls stacked together on one hand.

## HEADBANGER

Elmer Cleve is seen here playing a tune on Charles Cheer's head. The human xylophone could form different notes by opening and closing his mouth.

OOOF!

# SECRET AGENTS

## Milk Bottle Makeover

Residents of Stourbridge in England were surprised when they discovered doorstep delivered bottles intricately etched with cows, sheep, and mice alongside their morning milk. Now the person who secretly deposited these works of art has been revealed as local glass museum artist Charlotte Hughes-Martin.

## Guerrilla Gardener

The harsh winter of 2010 left Britain's roads pitted with potholes and its cyclists covered with bruises. London bike rider Steve Wheen decided to transform the ugly holes into tiny gardens, planted with colorful flowers, to alert other road users. Sadly, the mini gardens were short-lived—one survived for three weeks but others fell victim to the traffic within hours.

### SAY WHAT!

An Icelandic designer has created a life-saving accessory for the well-dressed gentleman. His bullet-proof handkerchief, made of Kevlar, is intended to be worn in the breast pocket to protect the heart.

# Tooth Transmitter

Today's science fiction is often tomorrow's reality. People claim to have picked up radio broadcasts through fillings in their teeth, so a tooth implant containing a wireless receiver that transmits sound to the inner ear is not too farfetched. The audio implant, conceived by British art graduates James Auger and Jimmy Loizeau, appeared at London's Science Museum as part of a display of thought-provoking exhibits.

## ZOOM IN!

For another story about things that have appeared in unexpected places, check out the fishy tale on page 78.

# Shoe Conundrum

A Swedish couple hunting in the far north of Sweden stumbled upon 70 pairs of shoes, all filled with butter and placed at the top of a remote mountain. The mystifying scene was reminiscent of Beijing artist Yu Xiuzhen's photographic installation "Shoes with Butter" in which abandoned shoes full of butter lie by a pool in the Tibetan mountains.

FABULOUS FOLK

## Catalán Crusader

In 2009, local historian Lluis Colet spoke for five days and four nights on the subject of Spanish artist Salvador Dalí and Catalán traditions. Following his 124-hour speech at Perpignan station in southwest France, the 62-year-old dedicated his feat to those who defend the Catalán language and culture.

## Mole Man

When police searched Jose Del Rio's house in Austin, Texas, they discovered that he had dug a three-story network of tunnels beneath his home.

## Amazing Recovery

Indie band drummer Nicholas Blossom fell from a second-story balcony and impaled his head on a fence post spike. He was taken to the ER with part of the post still embedded in his scalp, yet was able to laugh and joke with his family after surgery.

## First-Grade Flier

Luan da Silva from Florianoplois, Brazil, is just six years old but he regularly straps on a specially weighted paragliding harness and takes to the skies. The intrepid young paraglider made his first flight with his instructor father at the age of two and his first solo flight a year later.

## Short Speech

In 1793, U.S. President George Washington gave his second inaugural address in the Senate Chamber of Congress Hall in Philadelphia. It was just 135 words long and lasted less than two minutes.

## First Lady

In 1979, women's civil rights leader Susan B. Anthony's image was chosen for the new dollar coin, making her the first woman to be depicted on U.S. currency.

## Bottle Nose

Judo champion Jemal Tkeshelashvili bursts hot water bottles by inflating them with his nose. It took the 18-year-old from Georgia, in the former Soviet Union, just 13 seconds to burst one bottle.

## Marathon Man

After taking part in three marathons during 2009, Japanese runner Keizo Yamada decided to retire at the age of 81. Yamada, who competed at the 1952 Olympics, says he will continue with his daily 12-mile jogs to stay in shape.

## See a Penny...

Craig Davidson of Phoenix, Arizona, always stops to pick up any coins he spots on his daily runs. The 54-year-old finds money virtually every day and has collected $8,100 in dropped coins over 25 years. The money has paid for a Hawaiian vacation for him and his wife.

## Child Genius

British toddler Karina Oakley was found to have an IQ of 160 at just two years old—the same as that of Microsoft chairman Bill Gates and physicist Stephen Hawking. Karina was tested by an educational psychologist and asked to complete challenges in verbal ability, memory, and numbers and shapes.

## Never Give Up

A 68-year-old grandmother from South Korea finally passed her written driver's license exam on her 950th attempt. Cha Sa-Soon had been taking the 50-minute test for four years and spent more than $4,000 on application fees. Now she just needs to pass the practical test.

## Power Prodder

In 2009, 56-year-old kung-fu master and street performer Ho Eng Hui from Malaysia used his right index finger to smash through the tough shells of four coconuts in little more than 30 seconds.

## Monk's Marathon

In 2009, 34-year-old Endo Mitsunaga became the 13th monk since World War II to complete the Sennichi Kaihogyo— 1,000 days of walking, meditation, and prayer around Mount Hiei, Japan. The Buddhist monk walked for 26 miles a day for periods of 100 or 200 days at a time, and covered a distance roughly equivalent to the Earth's circumference.

Former bodyguard Tiny Iron from London, England, has biceps that measure an incredible 24 inches in circumference—that's bigger than most people's thighs.

# WHY NOT?

## Kung Fu Coiffeur

Chinese hairdresser Wang Xiaoyu may have some tips for stylists who suffer from sore feet. Wang, who has had 18 years' training in kung fu, is making use of his martial-art skills to cut his clients' hair upside down while standing on his head.

### SAY WHAT!

Born in 1902, Malaysian centenarian Wook Kundor married her 23rd husband, who is 71 years her junior, in 2006. The couple are now talking about adopting a baby.

## Masked Ball

In Sydney, Australia, 74 scuba divers took to the floor of the 55-yard pool at the Olympic Park Aquatic Centre in an attempt to dance simultaneously underwater for at least 10 minutes while raising money for charity.

# Flying Dutchman

Dutch illusionist Ramana amazed the crowd in New York by levitating above the ground with no visible means of support. Some people think it is possible to levitate using just the power of the mind but, more often, it is a trick.

# Huge Headgear

The Nihangs, or Sikh warriors, wear conical blue or yellow turbans, which have great spiritual significance. Baba Balwant Singh took the style to its extreme at a Sikh festival in Amritsar with a turban weighing 130 pounds. The unwound cloth stretched 2,300 feet—140 times longer than the average turban and the length of seven football fields.

# PARTY TIME

## Chocolate-Covered

Music festival-goers often end up covered in mud, but visitors to the Sziget Festival in Budapest were offered a sweeter way to get dirty. Hungarian confectioner Tibi invited people to wrestle in a giant pool of chocolate. The prize for the champion wrestler was a selection of Tibi gifts—but the winner might have had enough of chocolate by then.

## Firework Frenzy

Visitors to the Beehive Rocket Festival in Yan Shui, Taiwan, go dressed in a helmet, face mask, gloves, and boots and take towels for extra protection. As spectators stand in the square, millions of firecracker rockets buzz through the air like angry bees, aiming directly at the crowd. Participants believe that being hit by a rocket will bring them good luck.

**SNIFF**

**ACHOO**

# Paintballing Indian-Style

The colorful Indian festival of Holi welcomes the spring and celebrates the triumph of good over evil. People smear each other with paint and throw colored powders at passersby. Some fill water pistols or syringes with colored water to attack from a safe distance and water bombs are popular weapons. Class and status are forgotten—once everyone is covered in paint there is no way of telling who is rich and who is poor, and even politicians get a thorough soaking.

TECHNO TALK

# BODY EXPERIENCE

## Taste the View

Lance Corporal Craig Lundberg, who was blinded by a grenade while serving in Iraq, is the first person to use BrainPort, a device that lets him "see" with his tongue. Images from a tiny video camera attached to a pair of sunglasses are converted to electrical pulses that are sent to his tongue via a plastic "lollipop."

### SAY WHAT!

We like to think that we are superior creatures, but an onion has a genetic code five times longer than that of a human being.

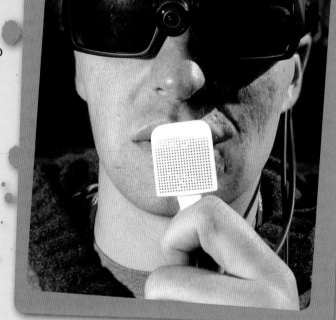

## Brain-Cooler

British motorcyclist Jullian Preston-Powers has invented the ThermaHelm, a helmet that could save many lives. The brain often swells following an accident and traditional helmets act like insulators, increasing its temperature. The ThermaHelm contains packs filled with water and ammonium nitrate, which mix together in the event of an impact, producing a cooling effect and reducing the chance of brain damage.

# Human Touchscreen

As devices like cell phones and MP3 players get smaller, their tiny touchscreens become increasingly difficult to use. A joint project between Carnegie Mellon University and Microsoft has come up with an unusual solution to this problem. "Skinput" makes use of a large surface that is always on hand. A mini projector attached to an armband turns your wrist into a screen or your hand into a calculator. The device has a sensor that recognizes which part of your body is being tapped and has been proved to be as accurate as a smartphone keypad.

Ripley's asked Chris Harrison, Skinput researcher, about the device. **Does it hurt?** Not at all. It requires about the same force as tapping on a regular touch screen, or on a table or friend's back. That's the great thing about your body—it actually conducts sound really well. Solids and liquids are many times better than air. Skinput works whereby the acoustics from the finger tap travel up the bone and soft tissues to the sensors located on the upper arm.

**As Skinput works with the use of a mini projector, does your arm have to be at a certain angle?** You do have to bring your arm to a particular posture, but future versions of the system will use a depth camera, so that the projection will track automatically with the arm. Imagine your iPod strapped to your arm while out for a run. To control the volume or song, you soon might just be able to tap your fingers or palm. I'm convinced that anything you could do on a device like an iPhone, you'll be able to do right on your palm.

55

# SPOOKY STUFF

## Who Ya Gonna Call?

GhostRadar has a sensor to detect small changes in electromagnetic turbulence when ghosts are nearby and will alert you to the presence of paranormal activity with an array of flashing lights and alarms. The product comes with a USB flash drive, which may not record supernatural phenomena, but will store your photos and other data.

## Ghostly Grimace

Santa Maria della Salute in Venice was built in the 17th century in honor of the Virgin Mary. Venetians believed she saved them from the Black Death, which had killed 50,000 people in the city. This photograph of a grim, ghostly face in the clouds above the basilica could be a reminder of the church's dark history.

# Odd App-Arition

A workman who was demolishing a school near Hull, northern England, downloaded some cell phone photos of the site to discover the ghostly image of a boy standing by the rubble. Although the builder insisted that the photograph was genuine, it has been suggested that one of his colleagues may have been playing a prank on him.

CREEPY!

## Weird World

A Buddhist temple in Thailand is offering the opportunity to be reborn. Visitors who wish to be resurrected lie in a coffin for a few minutes while monks chant death rites, then they rise to a new life.

A woman in Los Angeles started to see ghostly figures and experience strange events, such as lights and faucets turning themselves on and off, after she became pregnant.

The door to the grandfather clock in the Governor's Mansion in Nevada opens and shuts by itself and a woman in a white gown is sometimes seen walking nearby.

Travelers on Highway 58, east of Tehachapi, California, claim to have seen ghost pirates burying their treasure close to the rusty hull of the SS *Minnow*, the tour boat from the 1960s sitcom *Gilligan's Island*.

The Kawaiisu tribe believed that there were portals to the underworld in the Tehachapi mountains, where a deer spirit guided travelers through a window of water on a journey through the Earth's creation.

# BRIGHT SPARK

Dr. Peter Terren has combined a fascination with electricity and a love of photography to create an electrifying reconstruction of Rodin's sculpture *The Thinker*. Using a device called a Tesla coil, which boosts the power of electricity to generate a super-charged burst of energy, the Australian transformed himself into a human sparkler. Protected by a layer of insulating foil, he passed about 200,000 volts over his body. The electricity traveled through the foil and out to the earth from his foot.

Dr. Terren stuffed steel wool into one of his shoes to create a shower of sparks from his foot.

If a single spark got through the inventor's flimsy protection, it would throw him to the ground, like a shock from a Taser.

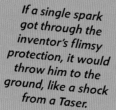

ANOTHER THINK COMING

## The Thinker

Created between 1879 and 1889 by Parisian artist Auguste Rodin, *The Thinker* is one of the world's most famous sculptures. The bronze figure was originally called *The Poet* and was meant to represent Italian poet Dante, contemplating his great work *The Divine Comedy*.

# OUT OF THIS WORLD

## "Tree" Trails

A camera on board the *Mars Reconnaissance Orbiter* has sent back pictures from the red planet that appear to show rows of conifers sprouting from sand dunes. In fact the "trees" are dark trails of debris caused by landslides, as the frozen carbon dioxide that coats the dunes melts during the Martian spring.

## To Infinity . . . and Back

*Toy Story*'s Buzz Lightyear returned to Earth aboard space shuttle *Discovery* following a mission to the International Space Station. The space ranger spent 467 days in orbit— 30 days longer than any other astronaut. He was participating in NASA's Toys in Space program.

# Lunar Timepiece

Swiss watchmaker Romain Jerome celebrated the 40th anniversary of the 1969 Moon landing by creating a watch with a face coated in dust from Moon rocks and a strap partly woven with fibers from an ISS spacesuit. The case contained material from the *Apollo 11* spacecraft.

## ANOTHER THINK COMING

- If the Sun suddenly stopped shining it would take eight minutes before we realized, because it takes that long for sunlight to reach the Earth.

- The Sun accounts for more than 99.8 percent of the total mass in the solar system. If it were hollow, more than 1.3 million Earths could fit inside it.

- The temperature at the Sun's core is more than 28 million degrees Fahrenheit and the pressure is so great that nuclear reactions occur constantly, creating 85 percent of its energy.

- The sun is middle-aged. It has existed for about 4½ billion years and it is expected to survive for another five billion.

# Radiant Rails

Nullarbor Plain, a vast, arid area in southern Australia, is crossed by the longest straight section of railroad in the world. Twice a year, the 297-mile stretch of track is aligned with the setting Sun, creating a stunning image.

APPLIANCE OF SCIENCE

## Mobile Home

Moving home could become a lot easier thanks to a walking house designed by Danish artists and engineers working in Massachusetts. The 10-foot-high solar-powered pod has six hydraulic legs, so it can walk away from floods—or even noisy neighbors.

## Gas Lake

There is enough methane beneath the surface of Africa's 1,500-foot-deep Lake Kivu to supply neighboring Rwanda with electricity for the next 400 years, but the gas, along with the carbon dioxide and hydrogen sulfide that are also trapped in the water, could kill the two million people living in the lake basin if it were to surface.

## Ringing Dress

British fashion student Georgie Davies has invented a dress that solves the problem of not being able to hear your cell phone in a crowded place. Translucent white scales on one shoulder of the dress are wirelessly connected to the wearer's phone and light up when it rings.

## Light Show

Mysterious lights have been appearing along the ridge of Brown Mountain, North Carolina, for more than 800 years. Scientific explanations, including swamp gases, mirages, and reflected headlamps, have all been discounted. The lights have been described as a glowing orb, a whirling pinwheel, and a bursting skyrocket, varying in color from white to green, orange, or violet.

## Texts or Toilets

More people in India have access to a cell phone than to a lavatory. Cell phone subscribers total 563.73 million—enough to serve about half the population—but only one third have access to proper sanitation.

## Too Many Teeth

Chelsea Keysaw of Kinnear, Wyoming, had three operations between the ages of 7 and 12 to remove 13 additional permanent teeth and 15 baby teeth.

## Eye-Watering Energy

Some people claim that it's possible to recharge an MP3 player by sticking the USB cable into an onion soaked in a sports drink. According to the theory, the electrolytes in the drink react with ions in the onion to create an electrical charge.

## Musical Microbes

*Waste-eating bacteria at a water treatment plant in Treuenbrietzen, Germany, are working more efficiently since the manager started playing Mozart's Magic Flute at the sewage center. The plant expects to save over $1,000 a month thanks to the increase in microbial activity.*

## Missile Power

*Russian nuclear missiles that may once have been aimed at the U.S.A. are now being used to provide electricity for the country's homes. Fuel from dismantled nuclear weapons, including those from the former U.S.S.R., is used to generate about ten percent of the electricity produced by American power plants.*

## Rainmaker

*Under certain atmospheric conditions a plane traveling through clouds can cause a narrow band of rain or snow to fall, leaving a hole or channel in the clouds.*

## Justice-Seeking Specter

*Zona Heaster Shue was thought to have died as the result of a fall at her home in Greenbrier County, West Virginia, in 1897. However, four weeks after her burial, Zona's ghost appeared to her mother and described how her husband Edward had killed her. Her body was exhumed and an autopsy revealed that she had been strangled. Edward was convicted and sentenced to life imprisonment.*

## Bird vs. Broadband

*People complaining about their broadband speeds may joke that it would be faster to send the data by carrier pigeon, but a company in South Africa has proved that it is true. A pigeon took one hour eight minutes to carry a 4GB memory stick 60 miles and it then took an hour to upload the data. Meanwhile just four percent of the data had been transferred using the country's leading Internet service provider.*

## Match Days

*The dates 4/4, 6/6, 8/8, 10/10, and 12/12 always occur on the same day of the week as the last day of February. Date pairs 5/9 and 9/5, as well as 7/11 and 11/7, also fall on the same day.*

# SUM THING WEIRD

Mathematician Srinivasa Ramanujan was visited in the hospital by a colleague who said, "I came here in cab number 1729 ... a very dull number."

"It's quite interesting," Ramanujan replied immediately. "It is the smallest number that can be expressed as the sum of two cubes in two different ways." ($1729 = 1^3 + 12^3$ and $9^3 + 10^3$)

Choose any prime number greater than 3 (e.g. 23). Square that number ($23 \times 23 = 529$). Add 14 ($529 + 14 = 543$). Divide by 12 ($543/12 = 45$ with remainder 3). The remainder will always be 3! If you add 17 instead of 14, the remainder will always be 6.

$1{,}741{,}725$ equals $1^7 + 7^7 + 4^7 + 1^7 + 7^7 + 2^7 + 5^7$

The number $111{,}111{,}111$ multiplied by itself equals $12{,}345{,}678{,}987{,}654{,}321$

When the teacher asked future mathematician Carl Friedrich Gauss and his class to add all the numbers from 1 to 100 together, he had the answer in 30 seconds. He realized that if you add 1 to 100 you get 101, $2 + 99$ is also 101, and so on until you get to $50 + 51$. Therefore he just multiplied 101 by 50 to get 5050.

19 equals $1 \times 9 + 1 + 9$
29 equals $2 \times 9 + 2 + 9$
This works for all two-digit numbers ending in 9 up to 99

Pick any 3-digit number (e.g. 273)
Repeat the number (i.e. 273,273)
Divide by 7 ($273{,}273/7 = 39{,}039$)
Divide by 11 ($39{,}039/11 = 3{,}549$)
Divide by 13 and you get your original number ($3{,}549/13 = 273$)

# Rubik's Cube Facts

○ A standard Rubik's Cube has six colored sides, 21 pieces, and 54 outer surfaces. This means there are 43,252,003,274,489,856,000 possible configurations.

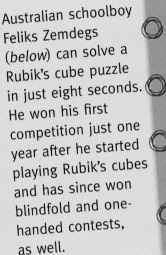

Australian schoolboy Feliks Zemdegs (*below*) can solve a Rubik's cube puzzle in just eight seconds. He won his first competition just one year after he started playing Rubik's cubes and has since won blindfold and one-handed contests, as well.

○ If every configuration of a single Rubik's square were lined up, they would cover the Earth 276 times.

○ Ernö Rubik invented the Cube in 1974. The Hungarian architect and professor first called it the "magic cube."

○ If you turned one of the its faces every second, it would take 1,400 million million years to go through every possible configuration of the cube.

○ People compete to solve the cube blindfolded, one-handed, and with their feet.

○ In 1995, the Masterpiece Cube was created for Rubik's 15th birthday. It was made of 18-carat gold encrusted with 22.5 carats of amethyst, 34 carats of rubies, and 34 carats of emeralds. Its estimated value was 1.5 million dollars.

# UNDER THE KNIFE

## Eyes Wide Open

This picture shows Swaroup Anand undergoing open-heart surgery in Bangalore while he is wide awake. The 23-year-old has been given an injection of anesthetic in his neck to numb his body. It means that doctors can ask him to cough or take a deep breath during the operation, and he won't suffer the after-effects of a general anesthetic, so he can leave the hospital earlier.

### Insider Knowledge
The human body contains trillions of cells, but these are outnumbered by at least ten to one by the number of bacteria living within the body.

## Sharp Practice

Professional sword swallower Chayne "Space Cowboy" Hultgren amazed a crowd in Sydney, Australia, by swallowing 18 swords at once. It takes many years to master this deadly art. Performers must first overcome their natural gag reflex, then learn to keep their swallowing muscles open, and finally maneuver their internal organs to allow the sword a smooth passage. Chayne has been stretching his throat using hoses since he was 16 and has a particularly low stomach, enabling him to swallow longer blades than usual.

# Best Foot Forward

Jingle Luis put the soles of her feet on the floor for the first time at the age of 15. Jingle, from the Philippines, was born with feet that were twisted backward and upside down. Doctors in New York inserted screws into the bones of her feet and turned them a little each day for six weeks until Jingle's feet were rotated into the correct position.

## SAY WHAT!

When Israel Sarrio's arm was torn off in a traffic accident, doctors in Valencia, Spain, sewed the severed limb to his leg to keep it alive until it could be reattached.

# MEDICAL MARVELOUS

## Boa Buddy

For most people, wrapping a boa constrictor around their necks means dicing with death, but Daniel Greene's pet, Redrock, keeps him safe. Somehow the five-foot snake senses when the epilepsy sufferer from Shelton, Washington, is about to have a seizure and gives him a little squeeze so he can take his medication or lie down in a suitable place.

## Bendy Bette

After teaching yoga for over 40 years, Bette Calman can still strike a pose that most people a quarter her age would find impossible. The 83-year-old grandmother from Williamstown, southeast Australia, claims that she is more flexible now than 50 years ago and has no plans to give up.

### SAY WHAT!

After suffering a stroke, Gisela Leibold has motion blindness. She cannot see movement and everything appears to her as a series of freeze frames.

# Grin or Bear It

The Happiness Hat, designed by interactive artist Lauren McCarthy, is the perfect headgear for customer service personnel on a wet Monday morning. The hat has a sensor that attaches to your cheek and detects whether you are smiling. If not, a metal spike jabs you in the back of the head.

# Nil by Mouth

Kaleb Bussenschutt has never enjoyed a slice of birthday cake or eaten a piece of fruit. The five-year-old from Australia is allergic to all foods and can only swallow water and lemonade. He has a nutritious formula feed pumped directly into his stomach and, when the family goes out to eat, Kaleb gets a cup of ice so he has something to chew.

# HOME SWEET HOME

## Best Bus Stop

The remote Scottish island of Unst, which is home to 700 people, has the officially recognized Best Bus Shelter in Britain. The luxurious shelter is fully carpeted and has been fitted out with a TV, a computer, a radio, and even a microwave. It is regularly refurbished and was given a soccer-themed makeover in celebration of the 2010 World Cup.

## Vampire Nightlight

This might be the perfect lamp for Count Dracula's bedside table. Designer Mike Thompson has come up with a light powered by blood. Users break off the top of the single-use glass lantern and cut their fingers on the jagged edge. When the blood is mixed with a special tablet it makes the lamp glow.

### SAY WHAT!

Trimming the top of a seven-foot hedge can be a chore, so a New Zealand man decided to do the job with his ride-on lawnmower, which he hoisted onto the hedge using a crane.

# Moving House

This house in eastern England looks like a timber clad barn until the sun comes out and it reveals its secret. The wooden outer shell glides back to expose an inner house made of glass. When it gets too hot, the shell slides back to provide shade. The outer house travels at 0.2 mph and beeps to warn people it's on the move.

# Baby Bot

Researchers at Tokyo University are using a robot baby, named Noby, to study child development. Noby has been programmed to behave like a nine-month-old. He has 600 sensors across his body so he can feel touch, while cameras and microphones in his head allow him to see and hear.

# MAD INVENTIONS

## Robot Chaplain

It looks like a traditional wedding, but when Tomohiro Shibata and his bride Satoko Inoue tied the knot in Tokyo all the attention was on the officiant, as the ceremony was conducted by a robot named i-Fairy. The bride works for the company that makes the four-foot robot and her husband is a professor of robotics.

## Clever Jell-O

A British company has developed an intelligent orange gel that could replace bulky protective padding. Called d3o, the material is soft, like putty, but hardens to absorb the force of any impact before going back to its Jell-O-like state. It was developed for body armor, but is also ideal for protective sportswear and cases for cell phones and laptops.

# Charge as You Dance

Power wellies may be the answer to two common problems among music festival-goers—wet feet and dead batteries. The boots have a power-generating sole that converts heat from feet into power for cell phones and MP3 players. Twelve hours' walking produces one hour of battery life, but dancing or running will generate electricity more quickly.

orange

## ZOOM IN!

If you think these garments will make you stand out in a crowd, take a look at the weird creations on pages 98–99.

ZZZZ...

# Woolly Wackiness

If you don't want someone checking out your Facebook page over your shoulder, the Body-Laptop Woolly Sweater is perfect for providing your own personal space and giving you protection from prying eyes when out in public. Beware of overheating though.

# WONDERFULLY WEIRD

# SUPER-HUMANS

## Pop-Up!

Jalisa Thompson has been able to "pop" her eyes since the age of 9, but she wasn't on the Ripley's radar until 2006, when she won the Funny Face Contest at the Ripley's Museum in Atlantic City, New Jersey. She can pop out each eye a full half inch out of its socket—and is able to do one at a time or both simultaneously! She enjoys the surprised and shocked reactions her incredible talent provokes.

## Puzzling Protrusion

The family and friends of Chinese grandmother Zhang Ruifang were baffled when the 101-year-old sprouted a goatlike horn from her forehead. The 2.4-inch growth took a year to reach its current size and is thought to be a cutaneous horn made of keratin—a protein found in skin, hair, and nails.

# Two-Foot Teen

Indian teenager Jyoti Amge is tinier than a toddler and weighs just 12 pounds. The schoolgirl is proud of her size—people in her hometown of Nagpor treat her like a mini-celebrity and some even regard her as a goddess. Jyoti suffers from a form of dwarfism and will never grow any taller, yet, despite her small stature, she has big ambitions. She has already released an album with bhangra/rap star Mika Singh and dreams of becoming a Bollywood star.

## ZOOM IN!

Small size, big attitude exists throughout the animal kingdom too. Check out pages 128–129.

# WHAT ARE THE CHANCES?

## Dog Eats Cats

When Snowy, a West Highland terrier from Cambridgeshire, England, stopped eating, the veterinarian took an X-ray and was amazed to find a family of five cats in her stomach. The dog had swallowed the five pottery ornaments several weeks earlier.

## Flying Fish?

A four-foot-high chain-link fence studded with fish might make you wonder, but these guys were swept through the streets of Orange, Texas, on a tide of seawater when Hurricane Ike battered the state in 2008. When the waters receded, residents were amazed to find that the fence had become a giant fishing net.

# Buddhist Blooms

A Chinese nun has discovered rare udumbara flowers underneath her washing machine. According to Buddhist legend, the tiny flower, which measures just a fraction of an inch, blooms only once every 3,000 years and it is said to mark the arrival of a new king.

## SAY WHAT!

A father searching for his long-lost daughter made an appeal in a local newspaper. His daughter saw her father's photograph and, on closer inspection, spotted herself in the background.

# Wedding on Wheels

A wedding can be a moving occasion, especially for couples who tie the knot in the Best Man mobile wedding chapel. The vehicle is a 1942 American la France truck belonging to ordained minister Darrell Best from Shelbyville, Illinois. It travels at speeds up to 55 mph and is fitted with stained-glass windows, a pipe organ, an altar, and two wooden pews.

# THAT'S GOTTA HURT

## Hook Up

Performers at a festival in Jiaxing, eastern China, demonstrate their strength by hanging heavy weights from hooks in their skin. Hindu devotees go even further during the Thaipusam Festival and pull heavy chariots fastened to hooks attached to the skin of their backs, while some performance artists suspend their whole bodies from deep-sea fishing hooks in their chests or backs.

## Live Wire

Chewing on electrical wiring is not normally a good idea, as many mice and rats have found out. However, Wang Ailing entertained the viewers of a TV show in Zhengzhou, China, by biting straight through an electric cable.

# Heavyweight Massage

A shiatsu barefoot massage is the latest health craze to hit the spas, but imagine if the masseuse about to walk on your back turned out to be a three-ton elephant. Surprisingly, tourists in Thailand are queuing up to find out what it's like to be trodden on by the world's largest land animal.

# King of the Stingers

Nettle noshers from around the world gather each year at a village in Dorset, southwest England, for the Stinging Nettle Eating Championship. Competitors eat the leaves from two-foot-long stalks, then the bare stems are measured and the winner is crowned. Nettle leaves are covered in thousands of microscopic hypodermic needles that inject stinging chemicals into the skin.

# PLANE AMAZING

British TV presenter James May wanted to prove that traditional toys are still as much fun as ever by using them to create supersized projects. One of his challenges was to build a full-sized model of a World-War-II Spitfire fighter plane, using an Airfix plastic model kit. The kit was delivered in 25 parts, complete with a plastic pilot, and assembled and painted with the help of schoolchildren at RAF Cosford in England, where the original aircraft were built.

ANOTHER THINK COMING

## Little Fighter

The Spitfire was a single-seater fighter plane that was used throughout World War II. Much loved by its pilots, the Spitfire became a legend following its impressive performance during the Battle of Britain in 1940, when the British Air Force fought the German Luftwaffe in the skies above southern England.

# DEAD STRANGE

## Sleep with the Fishes

Divers are flocking to an underwater cemetery off the coast of Miami that is modeled on the lost city of Atlantis. The man-made reef is home to thousands of fish and the remains of hundreds of people. The ashes of those who want to be buried 40 feet under are mixed with cement and molded into shapes such as starfish or shells before being committed to the deep.

## SAY WHAT!

Actress Sarah Bernhardt sometimes practiced her lines and slept in a coffin to help her understand her tragic roles.

Passengers on a train in Germany called the police when they mistook a sleeping Halloween reveler dressed as a zombie for a murder victim.

"It's Great to be Alive in Colma!" is the motto of a Californian town where the population of 1,500 is outnumbered by 1.5 million deceased residents, most of whom were relocated from San Francisco.

Rural Chinese families sometimes buy the body of a woman to bury with their dead unmarried sons so they have a wife in the afterlife.

## Funky Funeral

Some people wouldn't be seen dead in such a wacky wagon, but for the Sixties generation this psychedelic hearse could be the perfect transport to their final resting place. English businessman Matthew Shuter, who came up with the idea and suggests it would also be the perfect vehicle for festival-goers or for carrying surfboards.

GROOVY

# Final Ride

When British BMW-fan Steve Marsh passed away, his family decided to mark his passion with a scale-model of a BMW M3 convertible made from granite. The unusual headstone weighs about a ton and has a personalized license plate reading Steve 1. A family member even once placed a parking ticket on the windshield.

# 2-D Dad

When British dad-of-two Paul Challis sadly died at the age of 38, his wife wanted to keep his memory alive for their young children so she had a life-size cardboard cut-out made to "live" with the family. The cut-out attended Paul's funeral and was a guest at a friend's wedding a few weeks later. He was dressed up as Dracula on Halloween and as Santa at Christmas.

# PIECES OF ATE

## The Grazing Diet

After watching a TV show that claimed people can survive for ten days without eating, Li Sanju from Niwuei, China, decided to live on grass, roots, and leaves. After following his new diet for two years, Li feels fitter than ever and tumors on his leg have vanished.

## Food to Die For

Once a busy tea stall, the New Lucky Restaurant in Ahmadabad, India, has expanded into a nearby cemetery and customers now enjoy their tea and buns at tables set among the coffins of the departed.

## Fridge Raider

Despite taking regular exercise and following a low-fat diet, Anna Ryan from Missouri, U.S.A., continued to pile on the pounds. When she woke up to find her sheets covered in crumbs, she realized that she had been eating in her sleep. Cameras revealed that she was visiting the kitchen up to eight times a night.

## Looney Tunes

Princess Alexandra of Bavaria used to walk along the palace corridors sideways because she was convinced that she had swallowed a glass grand piano when she was a child.

## Night Wanderers

Sleepwalking often runs in families and it is more common in children. No one knows the cause, but it happens more often when people are overtired or stressed. Sleepwalkers have driven cars, cooked meals, and even committed murders.

## She's Cracked It!

One woman claims she has cured all her ailments by eating 50 eggshells a day for 13 years. Zhou Yuqin from Chongqing, China, says the fragile fragments are delicious and has convinced her daughter and son to eat them, too.

## Totally Gross

Scientists in the Amazon rainforest were shocked to find that two-toed sloths, which normally feed on plants, were scooping the human waste from their latrine and eating it.

## Dogs' Dinners

Francis Henry Egerton, the eighth Earl of Bridgewater, gave dinner parties for his dogs. Dressed in the latest fashions, his canine companions were served by servants from silver dishes and wore white napkins around their necks.

## Weird Wedding Fare

Wedding cakes date back to Roman times when a cake made of barley was broken over the bride's head. In the Middle Ages, newlyweds tried to kiss across a towering stack of buns, symbolizing a life of prosperity. Bride pie, which became popular in the 17th century, included cockscombs, lambs' testicles, and oysters—and some cooks even suggested adding live birds or a snake.

## Soil Snack

In Tuban, East Java, ampo is a traditional snack made from clean, gravel-free earth. Although there is no medical evidence, villagers believe that the snack is an effective painkiller and pregnant women are encouraged to eat it, as it is thought to refine the skin of an unborn baby.

## Medicinal Mummies

In the 12th century, doctors thought that powdered mummified bodies could cure everything from bruises and fractures to migraines and poisoning. In France, the mummies were boiled and their oil was skimmed off for use as a medicine.

## Feast Fit for a Sun King

French king Louis XIV, who lived from 1638 to 1715, was famous for his huge appetite. A typical belt-busting lunch, called "the little service," consisted of:

Four different bowls of soup
Whole, stuffed pheasant
Partridge, chicken, or duck
Mutton with garlic gravy
Two pieces of ham
Hard-boiled eggs
Three heaping salads
Plate full of pastries
Fruits and jams

Japanese food sculptor Takashi Itoh has been carving amazing art in watermelons for seven years. Entirely self-taught, he became an expert in just three weeks. His carvings include dragons, slogans, and Japanese cranes and tortoises. According to Takashi, you can carve many different fruits and vegetables as well as watermelons. He recommends using papayas, pumpkins, carrots, and the Japanese radish.

# OPEN THE ALBUM

## HAND-CARVED HOME

Lino Bueno could not afford to rent a house, so he carved one out of rock. It took 22 years to complete and included built-in benches, shelves, stairs, and a fireplace. The Spanish government rewarded his efforts by giving him the five-acre plot surrounding the house.

**GET DOWN!**

## MUSICAL EYEBROWS

Dancing eyebrows are a popular Internet phenomenon, but this man's eyebrows could dance to their own tune. F.G. Holt from Arkansas attached small bells to his eyebrows, as seen in this photo from 1941.

## READY TO TEAR

While paper clothes were a short-lived trend in the 1960s, this photograph from 1936 shows that they have been around for far longer. These two ladies are wearing coats made from copies of the Florida Times newspaper.

## BIG BEARD

After winning a competition for the longest beard in the 1860s, Edwin Smith continued to grow his beard until it measured eight feet. The gold miner had to employ a servant to wash and comb it.

## HIGH FLIERS

These acrobats are performing on a real flying trapeze. The wires supporting them both are suspended from a plane, flying high above the ground, and the girl is holding the man's feet using just her own feet.

Gus Simmons'

## CHILLY CHEEKS

In 1933, Gus Simmons won a prize after sitting on a two-foot cube of ice for 27 hours and 10 minutes. Unfortunately, he was later disqualified when he was found to have a fever of 102°F.

CONTEST

# DEATH CHEATERS

## Narrow Escape

A Chinese boy's ears saved his neck when he fell from an eighth-story window. Ming Ming's ears got caught between the bars of the window grille leaving him dangling nearly 100 feet above a city street. His screams alerted passersby and firemen forced the bars open so they could pull the six-year-old to safety.

### SAY WHAT!

A driver had a miraculous escape when a tanker pushed her car sideways along the road at 60 mph. The truck driver could not see the small car that had become trapped under his fender.

## Not so Funny

Funny-car driver Ron Dudley was lucky to survive when his car turned into a fireball as he crossed the finish line during a qualifying session at Indianapolis Raceway Park in 1987. Funny cars are high-performance dragsters that have bodies similar to street cars. Their large rear wheels make them tilt forward so they look "funny."

PHEW

ZOOM IN!

Humans aren't the only ones to have lucky escapes. Take a look at pages 124–125 to meet some animals that survived against the odds.

# Close Call

A lucky driver escaped injury when his car smashed through the seventh-floor wall of a parking garage in downtown Tulsa, Oklahoma. The 67-year-old Oklahoma man said his foot got stuck between the brake and gas pedals as he was backing into a space. He managed to stop the Mercedes just in time, leaving the trunk hanging in midair, but the owners of the cars in the parking lot over 80 feet below were less fortunate as bricks rained down on their vehicles.

# GOOD SPORTS

## Cuddly Caddy

At Sherwood Forest Golf Course, North Carolina, llamas are being trained to carry golfers' bags. The four-legged caddies may not be able to advise on the best club to use, but at the same time they won't criticize players' swings or comment on their embarrassing choice of golfing pants!

## The Big Pull

It took 16 workers six weeks and a massive load of rice straw to make the 600-foot-long rope for the Naha giant tug-of-war. Up to 15,000 people take part in the battle between east and west Naha, Japan. According to legend, if the east wins they will enjoy good health and happiness; if the west wins, they'll have a good harvest and prosperity.

# Clever Climber

Thirteen-year-old Maiko Kiesewetter from Hamburg combined his skill at darts and his love of climbing when he scaled a 16-foot-high wall. Maiko, who hopes to become a stunt man when he is older, used the darts he had thrown at the wooden wall to support himself as he climbed.

# Best of Both Worlds

The 8,300-ton soccer field at Sapporo Dome in Japan glides in and out of the stadium like a magic carpet, making way for a baseball diamond and a concert venue. The city gets 20 feet of snow a year so the grass needs protection from the harsh weather, but the system allows it to slide outside to benefit from the sunshine, too.

# AT YOUR DESK

## Centenarian Schoolgirl

Proving you're never too old to learn, a Chinese grandmother attended school for the first time at the age of 102. Ma Xiuxian needed to use a hearing aid and magnifying glass when she joined first-graders at elementary school in Shandong province. The mother of nine never had a chance to go to school and worked in a cotton mill from the age of 13.

## Mini Metropolis

This urban sprawl of silver skyscrapers, called Ephemicropolis, is made from 100,000 staples. It took Peter Root 40 hours to painstakingly position the building-like stacks on the floor of an office block on the island of Guernsey, in the English Channel. The artist and part-time lecturer is now planning an even bigger cityscape using one million staples.

# High School Run

Carrying her younger brother in a sack, nine-year-old Daisy Mora (*below, left*) ziplines along half a mile of steel cable at speeds up to 40 mph to get to school. For families living in a remote Colombian mountain village the 12 cables spanning the raging Rio Negro, 1,300 feet below, are their only access to the outside world.

# Apple or Pair?

Your lunchbox would be extra nutritious if it contained these twin apples. The strange mirror-image fruits were found by a farmer in Presov, Slovakia. Conjoined fruits are rare and are thought to be caused by cold weather, fluctuations in temperature, or insect damage.

# GET CREATIVE!

# GLAD RAGS

## From Sneaker to Slip-On

When the weather looks unsettled, or suitcase space is limited, the German-designed Nat-2 shoes could be the answer to everyone's footwear dilemmas. In just a flick of the zipper, the two-in-one shoes transform from sneakers to sandals. There are more than 20 different designs and the tops of the shoes are interchangeable so you can mix and match the soles with different uppers.

## Eye Catcher

Kevin Carter, a special-effects artist who works on Hollywood blockbusters, was originally employed in his dad's optometry business. Now he has combined both specialties to produce a range of scary contact lenses. Each lens takes up to two days to hand paint and they have clear centers so the wearer can still see.

# DIY Dress

No one will turn up in an identical outfit to the Color-In Dress. The black-and-white frock comes with a set of textile markers so the owner can fill in the print to personalize the design. The wearable coloring book would be the perfect way to while away the time at a boring event or during a long journey.

# Face of Fashion

Try getting creative with the crumpled clothes on your bedroom floor. New York-based artist Bela Borsodi turns sleeves into eyes and collars into mouths with his outfit origami. Bela spent four days creating the striking Fashion Faces as part of an advertising campaign for an online fashion retailer.

# SMALL OFFERINGS

## On a Roll

French artist Anastassia Elias creates tiny dioramas inside cardboard toilet-paper tubes. She spends hours carefully cutting tiny shapes from cardboard to make detailed models, and then fits them inside the rolls using tweezers. Her cut-out creations come to life when a light is shone through the tube, silhouetting the scene.

## Minuscule Models

Dough figure sculpting is one of China's oldest traditional handicrafts. The dough is made from flour, honey, lard, and sugar, and some figurines are so highly detailed they include eyelashes, teeth, and fingernails. These tiny sculptures, which are small enough to fit inside a walnut shell, were made by 70-year-old dough figurine master He Xiaozheng.

# Teeny Train

This working train set is way smaller than a fingernail and includes a five-car train that is 35,200 times smaller than normal. Train enthusiast David Smith is building a village as part of his larger train set at home in New Jersey and the tiny train will be displayed in the window of the village's model shop.

## SAY WHAT!

You would need an electron microscope to read Teeny Ted from Turnip Town. Twenty copies of the book, produced by a Canadian nanotechnology lab, would fit on the head of a pin.

# Nano Snowman

Physicists have created a snowman that is about a fifth of the width of a human hair. It is made from two tiny tin beads that are normally used to calibrate electron microscope lenses, using tools designed for manipulating nanoparticles. An ion beam carved the eyes and smile and added a blob of platinum for a nose.

# THE BIG PICTURE

## Pin-free Zone

Forget poodles and elephants, competitors at the Balloon Art World Challenge in Bangkok create massive dragons, warriors on horseback, and even a copy of Andy Warhol's portrait of Marilyn Monroe. More than a million balloons are used during the international contest.

## Brick Master

Professional LEGO® artist Sean Kenney has built a seven-foot-wide model of the Nintendo DSi using 51,324 bricks. He spent 20 hours designing the sculpture, which weighs over 250 pounds. Sean has been a LEGO® fanatic since the age of four. He uses normal, off-the-shelf LEGO® pieces and keeps about 1.25 million bricks in his studio, all arranged by size, shape, and color.

# Making the Cut

The eerie tale *The Legend of Sleepy Hollow* by Washington Irving makes the Hudson Valley north of New York the natural home of Halloween. Each year the historic Van Cortlandt Manor in Croton-on-Hudson hosts the Great Jack-o'-Lantern Blaze. About 1,000 volunteers start preparing more than 4,000 hand-carved jack-o'-lanterns as early as June. The exhibits include those shown here: a near-lifesize Triceratops made from dozens of pumpkins, and eerie skeletal hands, as well as the Halloween classics of ghosts, goblins, and ghouls.

## SAY WHAT!

Meteorologists were amazed when a helium balloon released at a school fair in Manchester, northern England, was found 6,000 miles away in Guangzhou, China.

103

# WHAT'S THE BUZZ?

## Elfin Entomology

Pétra Werlé uses chewed bread to mold the faces and limbs of her elflike sculptures. Their bodies are made from butterflies, moths, beetles, feathers, and even the remains of shellfish dinners. The French artist displays her fairytale figures in bell jars, like scientific exhibits.

### SAY WHAT!

In 1997, four species of trilobites were named after members of the Ramones: Mackenziurus johnnyi, Mackenziurus joeyi, Mackenziurus deedeei, and Mackenziurus ceejayi.

## Winging It

Kung fu master Chen Pengxian used special breathing techniques to stop his hand shaking while he carved Chinese characters on a fly's wing. The sentence, which translates as "I am at the bottom of her valley of no love" is taken from his favorite martial-arts novel.

# High Fliers

Magnus Muhr has given new life to the dead flies that collect on his windowsill. The Swedish artist uses tiny tweezers to position the insects, then doodles around them and photographs the humorous scenes. The flies are shown engaging in all sorts of activities from sunbathing and horse riding to dancing and performing acrobatics.

**OWWW!**

**ZOOM IN!**

Insects are a pretty unusual medium to work with, but turn to pages 108–109 for some other wacky ways to create art.

# Jiminy Jackson

Mexican artist Enrique Ramos is no stranger to weird media. His representation of *The Last Supper* was woven from 22 pounds of spider webs, his portrait of Eminem was created in M&M's®, and other strange canvases include bats and butterflies. Now he has immortalized the late Michael Jackson on a series of edible Mexican crickets.

## "Just Asking"

**How does he do that?**
Enrique uses a three-haired brush and wears two pairs of glasses, one over the top of the other.

He shellacs the bugs to harden them before painting, but legs can still break off easily.

It takes about an hour to paint a cricket and that includes drying time between colors.

# FACE THE MUSIC

## Rock the Boat

Josh Pyke made waves in Sydney Harbour when he cruised through the waters in a giant guitar. The Australian singer-songwriter was filming a video clip for his single "Make You Happy." The boat, christened SS *Maton* after the Australian guitar company, was later auctioned in aid of a charity literacy project.

AHOY

## Playing with Fire

Jazz pianist Yosuke Yamashita said goodbye to an old piano by setting fire to it. The Japanese musician donned a fireproof suit and played the burning piano on a beach in front of an audience of hundreds. After about ten minutes, the flames got the better of the instrument and it fell silent.

# What a Fiddle

A violinist from the south China city of Guangzhou has made a violin measuring fewer than two centimeters (0.7 inches). Chen Lianzhi used a 0.1 mm drill, maple wood as thin as a nail, and strings finer than a human hair to make the fiddly little fiddle. The violin has over 30 components and it can produce a sound, but it is very high-pitched because the strings are so short.

## SAY WHAT!

In 2006, a Stradivarius violin almost 300 years old was sold at Christie's in New York for $3.5 million. In 2008, a Russian businessman bought a rare violin by Giuseppe Guarneri for an estimated $7 million.

# Cool Vibes

The world's first playable piano made entirely of ice was displayed at the Snow Sculpture Art Expo in Harbin, northeast China. Visitors did not need to be musical maestros to tickle the icy ivories as it was programmed to automatically play a repertoire of 30 classic pieces.

# MANIC MEDIA

## Artistic Upcycling

Enno de Kroon reuses egg cartons to create portraits that change, or even disappear completely, as you view them from different angles. The Dutch artist calls his paintings "Eggcubism" and enjoys the fact that the viewer can interact with the faces rather than just staring at them head-on. It's an interesting alterative to just throwing your old egg cartons into the recycling bin.

## Auto Portrait

British artist Ian Cook steered about 50 remote control cars dipped in paint around a canvas the size of a three-story building to create this giant portrait of Formula One champion Lewis Hamilton. The motorsport fan got the idea when a girlfriend gave him a remote-control car and told him not to get paint on it.

108

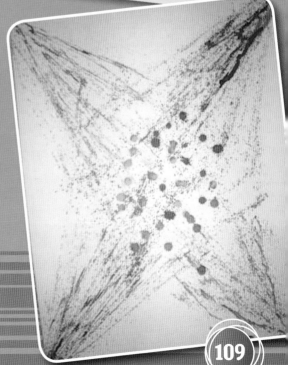

# Painting by Eye

Leandro Granato's technique of squirting and dripping paint onto canvases could have been inspired by famous American artist Jackson Pollock, but instead of using syringes and sticks, the Argentinian artist applies the paint with his eye. Leandro squirts paint up his nostril so it collects in his sinuses—small air pockets in the skull that are connected to the eyes. He then puts pressure on his nose to force the paint through his tear ducts and sprays it onto the canvas.

## SAY WHAT!

Alberto Cristini is a true water-colorist. Using a floating easel, the Italian artist has painted the Golden Gate Bridge and the Vancouver skyline while swimming in the sea.

# BUGS' LIFE

These beautiful patterns give a new twist to the word "culture." The images were created by Professor Eshel Ben-Jacob and his associates at Tel Aviv University. Although the colors and shading are artistic additions, the patterns themselves are formed by tens of billions of bacteria grown in a petri dish. Painting with microbes is not new—Alexander Fleming (1881–1955), who discovered penicillin, used to "paint" pictures in petri dishes using bacteria with different natural pigments.

## The Science Behind the Art

Professor Eshel Ben-Jacob tells us: "Each colony contains about 100 billion microorganisms—way more than the human population on Earth! And amazingly within each colony the bacteria send messages and communicate with each other at a highly intelligent level, in a system much like the Internet. This should not be surprising, as they did set the stage for all life on Earth.

"Some people ask why should we care about bacteria? Well, because they are our worst enemies and our best friends. They are our best friends because we couldn't live without them and our worst enemies because they have a resistance to antibiotics. This is why we must learn to understand the way they work and outsmart them."

# Bacteria Busted

Bacteria are single-celled microorganisms that are found everywhere on Earth. They can reproduce very quickly by splitting in two and may double their population every ten minutes. Not all bacteria are harmful—bacteria in soil help to break down organic material, while other bacteria help us to digest our food.

# BODY WORK

## Put on a Bold Face

Michigan artist James Kuhn discovered a passion for face painting when he was snowed in one day, so he decided to use his face as a canvas for 365 days running. The man of many faces came up with designs ranging from cartoon characters to his favorite foods during the year-long project.

### ZOOM IN!

Take a look at page 138 to see another creature that takes pride in its appearance.

## Human Flagpole

Guinness Rishi has over 200 national flags tattooed on his body, along with a map of the world across his stomach, and a tribute to *Ripley's Believe It Or Not!* on his forehead. The 67-year-old, from Dehli, India, is no stranger to extreme body modification—he had all his teeth removed so he could fit 755 drinking straws into his mouth.

# Tattoo-ine Tattoos

Dedicated *Star Wars* fan Luke Kaye was forced to sell a large part of his collection of memorabilia when it became too expensive to store, but the force will always be with him thanks to his extensive tattoos. Luke, from Swindon, England, has endured more than 100 painful hours under the needle to cover his back, arms, and legs with *Star Wars* images.

## SAY WHAT!

Thyroid cancer survivor Francesca Kaplan decided to memorialize her scar by creating a necklace in the same shape and now offers this service to others.

# Disney Devotee

George Reiger's skin is a testament to his love of all things Disney. The company's number one fan has over 1,900 Disney tattoos, which cover 85 percent of his body. His Disney-themed house in Pennsylvania is filled with over 19,000 Disney collector's pieces, he has celebrated six honeymoons at Disney parks, and when he dies, he wants his ashes scattered over the *Pirates of the Caribbean* ride.

# ARTISTIC LICENSE

## Big Cheese

Champion cheese carver Troy Landwehr worked for a week in a 40-degree cooler to sculpt the signing of the Declaration of Independence from a one-ton block of Cheddar in celebration of U.S. Independence Day on July 4, 2008.

## Ant Art

Artist Chris Trueman from Claremont, California, created a portrait of his younger brother using 200,000 dead harvester ants.

## Small Snippers

As well as creating an abacus less than half an inch high, and a model globe and china teapot less than a quarter of an inch high, Chen Yu Pei from China has made a working pair of stainless steel scissors just 0.068 inches long and 0.054 inches wide.

## In the Running

Sprinters raced through Tate Britain's central hall at 30-second intervals for four months in a tightly choreographed performance entitled "Work No. 850." The piece was devised by English artist Martin Creed.

## Memorial Teapot

John Lowndes from Pembrokeshire, Wales, enjoyed sharing a pot of tea with his dad so much that when his father died John had his ashes made into a teapot.

## Amazing Authors

Chen Hong suffers from a muscle disease that has left him unable to move or speak, yet he has written five novels with a total of 190,000 Chinese characters. The author dictates his books by blinking his eye when an assistant selects the correct symbol from a transparent board held above his head.

## Static Performance

Marina Abramovic sat still for over 700 hours as part of her 11-week exhibition entitled "The Artist Is Present." The Serbian artist sat silently at a table in New York's Museum of Modern Art while visitors took turns to sit opposite her.

## Valuable Vase

A lucky lady from Scotland who bought a second-hand vase for less than $2 was about to throw it away when a team from Antiques Roadshow arrived in town. Experts from the TV show recognized the vase as a 1929 piece by French designer René Lalique, and it later sold for almost $50,000.

## Wastelands

An eco-conscious British artist has created alternative uses for the dumpsters that clutter the streets of London. Oliver Bishop-Young has converted several containers into a park with a bench, a garden, a swimming pool, and a skateboard park.

## Picasso Poker

Art collector and casino mogul Steve Wynn was showing a Picasso painting to some friends when he accidentally put his elbow through the canvas. Wynn had been about to sell the painting, called Le Rêve, for $139 million but after having it repaired he decided to keep the picture.

## Unusual Talent

French naturalist and mollusk expert Baron de Ferussac (1786–1836) could recite any French or Latin poem backward after hearing it just once.

## Duct Tape Dress

Charis Hill was confident that no one would be wearing an identical dress when she attended her prom at Pamlico High, North Carolina. Charis had made her gown and matching sandals using five rolls of duct tape. She wore the leftover tape from the fifth roll as a bracelet in case she needed to do any emergency repairs during the evening.

Yellowdog was made by Herb Williams from Tennessee, who uses up to 250,000 coloring crayons to make some amazing sculptures. His studio is filled from floor to ceiling with boxes of colored crayons delivered directly from the manufacturer.

115

# EAT YOUR ART OUT

## Sweetmeats

The food on this tray looks good enough to eat, but take a closer peek before adding ketchup to the hot dog. Everything is the work of cake-designer Debbie Goard from San Francisco, who sculpts just about anything using cake and frosting. Her realistic-looking creations include dogs, cars, sneakers, and cell phones.

**WOOF!**

## No Dogs Allowed

Beijing artist Liu Wei has created a cityscape featuring the world's "tastiest" buildings, made entirely from dog chews. Entitled "Love It! Bite It!," the deserted city's cow-hide landmarks include the Pentagon, St. Peter's Cathedral, the Colosseum, and the Guggenheim art museum.

# Tasty Portrait

Malcolm West's portrait of screen icon Marilyn Monroe is made of thousands of jelly beans. It took the British artist six days to complete the four-foot-square mosaic and a day just to sort the beans into their different colors. The picture was displayed at a candy store where customers were asked to guess the number of beans used.

# Pumpkin King

Most people are happy to create jack-o'-lanterns with triangular eyes and noses and toothy grins, but Scott Cummins takes pumpkin carving to a new level. The art teacher from Perryton, Texas, sculpts detailed, 3-D faces in just an hour or two, using sharpened ice cream scoops, drill bits, potters' tools, and kitchen scourers. Sadly, his artworks soon find themselves in the compost bin.

117

CREATURE
FEATURES

# LOOKING GOOD

## Rodent Dog

Breeder of Cavalier King Charles spaniels, Nicoleta Piercy from Mesa, Arizona, is used to puppies with gorgeous coats, but when this little fella was born in 2009, he really caught her eye. With markings in the shape of the ears and head of Disney's most famous mouse, the pup could have only one name—Mickey.

## Froglight

The lights decorating the trees in James Snyder's backyard in Florida attract a lot of insects but this Cuban tree frog got more than it bargained for when it snapped up a bug sitting on a bulb. James noticed that the frog had swallowed the lamp and carefully removed it. The frog hopped away, none the worse for its light snack.

# Duck, Duck, Squash

At first glance this looks just like a duck preening its feathers, but it is actually a marrow grown in Somerset, England, and sculpted by nature. The two-inch stalk resembles a beak and there is an eyelike scar where the marrow scratched against a twig as it grew.

# Whiter Shade of Pale

This unusual albino alligator is part of a touring exhibition of reptiles, photographed in northern Germany. Meanwhile, in India, an even rarer white crocodile has lived alone since her birth in 1975 because she attacks any males released into her enclosure. Keepers at Bhitarkanika National Park have been searching for a suitable mate for the unsociable Gori for the past 18 years.

ANOTHER **THINK** COMING

## All White?

Albino animals are born with little or no pigment in their eyes, skin, and hair. They are at risk of getting sunburned and do not usually survive for long in the wild because they have no camouflage to conceal them from predators.

# BEHAVE YOURSELF

## Big Bird

Large groups of birds perform amazing, well-coordinated aerobatic maneuvers and often create fascinating patterns as the flock constantly changes shape. This photograph shows hundreds of thousands of spectacled teal taking on the form of a huge bird as they fly in formation above a lake in South Korea.

ZOOM IN!

For another story about strange animal behavior turn to page 134 and check out the rodeo rider with a difference.

## Fishy Tale

A goldfish named Jor Jor has been trained by her owner to play the hand bells. Diane Rains from Wisconsin has taught the musical fish to pull a string attached to the bells with her mouth. The two-year-old pet, who apparently likes the notes F and D, plays along with Barbra Streisand songs and even joined in with a performance on the TV show *American Idol*.

# Belly Buster

The great swallower has huge jaws and an expandable stomach, but this seven-inch fish found off the coast of Grand Cayman clearly had eyes even bigger than its large belly. It had attempted to eat a snake mackerel over four times its own length, which burst out of the great swallower's balloonlike stomach.

# Caught in the Act

Staff at Etali Safari Park in South Africa were baffled when water kept disappearing from their hot tub. Plumbers couldn't find a leak, yet every night the jacuzzi was empty. The mystery was solved when a guest heard a slurping noise. The culprit was a thirsty elephant—nicknamed "Troublesome" because of her inquisitive nature—who was draining the tub each day.

SLURP!

# PLUCKY & LUCKY

## Not so Cunning

The lives of three fox cubs almost went down the drain when they got their heads stuck in a grate in Plainfield, Connecticut. Firefighters pried the storm drain cover up, but could not cut through the thick metal. An animal control officer finally managed to free the trio by soaping their heads with detergent and sliding them back through the holes.

## Freezing Feline

A cat survived for four weeks in a freezing cold food warehouse by eating frozen peas. Staff tried to capture the cat, nicknamed Frosty, but he stayed out of reach until an animal rescue officer tempted him into a humane trap with milk and cat treats. Frosty did not escape unscathed, however, as he lost his tail and the tips of his ears to frostbite.

# Baby Boom

There was a sudden increase in the shark population at Kelly Tarlton's Underwater World in New Zealand when a wound in a school shark's abdomen led to an early delivery. The pregnant mother was bitten by a larger shark and visitors were amazed to see babies escaping from the gash. The four premature pups were moved to a nursery tank to be raised by oceanarium staff and their mother's wound was stitched up. The young sharks (*right*) were later released into the wild.

## SAY WHAT!

A drunken horse was found in a swimming pool in Cornwall, southwest England, after gorging himself on fermenting apples. The pony, named Fat Boy, had escaped from nearby riding stables.

**ANIMAL ANTICS**

## Sight-Savers

Creatures from sea lions to brown bears may have their sight saved thanks to a German company that makes contact lenses for animals blinded by cataracts.

## Sticky Situation

When Jack Russell terrier Toby chewed up the morning mail at Gill Bird's home in Hampshire, England, the envelope glue and paper set like papier-mâché and stuck the mischievous dog's jaws together.

## Master Mimics

Australian lyrebirds can imitate almost any sound, including chainsaws, cell phones, car alarms, dogs barking, and babies crying, as well as the calls of many other birds and even the human voice.

## Mystery Monster

The White River Monster was first spotted in Newport, Arkansas, in 1915, when witnesses reported seeing a gray-skinned creature "as wide as a car and three cars long." Occasional sightings followed, and in 1971 Cloyce Warren took a photo of a 30-foot-long creature with a spiny backbone while fishing with friends. Despite this evidence, the monster has never been identified.

## Boozy Badger

When police arrived to remove a dead badger from a road near the town of Goslar, Germany, they discovered that the animal was actually just drunk from eating too many fermented cherries.

## Deep-Water Deer

Chad Campbell and Bo Warren were fishing in Chesapeake Bay when they spotted a whitetail deer swimming in water 80 feet deep about a mile and a half from the shore. The pair lassoed the deer and manhandled him onto the boat so they could return him to dry land.

## Long Lick

An adult giraffe's tongue is 18–20 inches long and blue-black in color.

## Tadpole Shower

Residents were mystified when tadpoles rained from the sky in Japan's Ishikawa Prefecture in June 2009. Waterspouts and strong winds have been known to carry small fish and amphibians inland, but the weather at the time was quite calm.

## Fish Mine

Li Huiyan of Chongqing, China, hired 30 villagers for six months to dig a 50-foot-deep hole in his kitchen because he rightly suspected that an underground river beneath his house was full of fish. Li installed a net across the river and regularly hauls out fish, which he sells to support his family.

## Bright Buffalo

For five years, Mo Zhaoguang from China's Hubei province argued with his wife over who had left the light on in their barn. Then Mo spent a night in the barn and discovered that his buffalo was the culprit. It was pulling the cord switch with its teeth when it was hungry or thirsty and turning the light off again to go back to sleep.

## Flush Puppy

Four-year-old Daniel Blair from Middlesex, England, decided that the family's week-old cocker spaniel needed a bath, so he put the dog in the lavatory and flushed him away. Plumbers located the tiny puppy in a waste pipe 20 yards from the house and nudged him toward a manhole so he could be rescued.

## Pampered Pooches

When dogs Chelsea, Darla, and Coco Puff needed a place of their own, their owner, Tammy Kassis of Riverside County, California, commissioned an 11-foot-tall doghouse costing $20,000. Now the pets relax in their own Victorian mini-mansion with heating and air conditioning, handmade curtains, fancy wallpaper, and a picket-fenced lawn. Next on the shopping list is a plasma TV, so they can watch their favorite program, Animal Planet.

## Mayfly Storm

In 2010, there was such a massive swarm of newly hatched mayflies around the Mississippi River near La Crosse, Wisconsin, that they were picked up by the local Doppler weather radar.

Super Pet has created the "Critter Cruiser" for pet hamsters who are bored with going round and round the wheels in their cages. The cruiser is a fully hamster-powered car that enables our furry friends to race around a specially designed track, going as fast or slow as they like.

# SMALL BLESSINGS

**GRRR!**

## Lethal Leaper

Don't be fooled by this tiny frog—you're looking at one of the most lethal amphibians on the planet. The phantasmal poison frog from Ecuador secretes a toxin that can kill anyone who touches it, but scientists hope it could one day save lives, as a chemical in its poison has been found to block pain 200 times better than morphine, without serious side effects.

### SAY WHAT!

You wouldn't expect more than a peep from these poisonous frogs, whereas the world's largest animal, the blue whale, has a call of 180 decibels—that's louder than a jet engine.

## Pint-Sized Pinto

A pinto stallion named Einstein weighed just six pounds and stood 14 inches small when he was born at the Tiz A Miniature Horse Farm in New Hampshire. The tiny horse, which is about the size of a toy poodle, is seven inches shorter than the average miniature foal.

# Popular Pet

Peanut may have been a tiny horse but he was a massive hit, especially in Canada, where he was voted the country's most amazing pet. Smaller than a car tire, Peanut traveled all over North America raising money for charity. Sadly, he died of a brain tumor in 2004.

# Baa-Aaah

This tiny black lamb is about the size of a Labrador puppy. Named Mathilde, she is an Ouessant sheep, also known as a Breton Dwarf, and will reach a height of just 18 inches at the shoulder. The breed comes from the Île d'Ouessant in Brittany, France, where the dwarf sheep have adapted to survive the tough conditions on the windswept Atlantic Coast.

# CRAWLY & CREEPY

## Smiley Spider

Perhaps we would feel differently about arachnids if they all had smiles like this happy-face spider from the rainforests of Hawaii. Scientists think that the spider, which is under threat of extinction, has developed the markings to confuse predators. It measures just one sixth of an inch long and lives under leaves.

## Fearsome Faces

They may look like monsters from outer space, but these are the heads of a human flea (*below left*) and a bee (*left*). Scientific photographer Steve Gschmeissner used a scanning electron microscope to magnify these mini beasts by up to a million times. Steve says he chose to photograph insects because of the incredible shapes and patterns making up their bodies.

# Master of Disguise

Can you spot anything on this leaf? Conny Sandland was mystified when she noticed that the leaves of her mango tree in Kuala Lumpur were being eaten. She searched the tree for clues but it wasn't until she spotted something moving on one leaf that she found the culprit— the virtually invisible caterpillar of the common baron butterfly.

## SAY WHAT!

Pompeii worms live in water with temperatures up to 176° F, close to hydrothermal vents in the Pacific Ocean. They have a coat of bacteria that may insulate them from the scalding heat.

## Cuddly Crustacean

It's hard to imagine a cute lobster, but this might be how it would look. This furry crustacean was discovered south of Easter Island in the South Pacific in waters over 7,500 feet deep. The hairs on its arms and legs trap bacteria, which might be food for the creature, or may help to filter out the toxins that spew out from vents in the seabed.

# SAFARI SCARE

Visitors to the Lion Safari Park in Johannesburg, South Africa, are warned to lock their doors, but the couple in this car ignored the advice—thinking that a lion couldn't possibly open a car door—and almost became lunch. A 300-pound young male lion managed to open the car door before its terrified occupants put their foot on the gas and sped off.

"They must have been panicking because they didn't drive off straightaway," said Richard Holden from Tewkesbury, England, who was in the car behind and who took these amazing pictures.

**1** The young lion takes the handle in its teeth.

2 It pulls at the door.

3 The couple freeze as the door opens.

4 The driver hits the gas and they make their escape.

PHEW!

# ACTION ANIMAL

## Monkey Business

When the cowboy is a monkey, his "horse" is a border collie, and the "cows" are sheep, you know that you're watching a rodeo show with a difference. Whiplash is a 21-year-old capuchin monkey rescued as a baby from a cage in Florida. His owner, Tommy Lucia, says that the monkey enjoys performing and makes sure his doggy steeds know who's boss. Once he's done for the day, it's back to the chuckwagon for a dinner of strawberries, pears, apples, and bananas.

## King of the Swingers

Usually, great apes are terrified of water, so the fact that Suryia, a seven-year-old orangutan from Myrtle Beach Safari, South Carolina, can swim for 20 feet unaided using his rudimentary "Borneo Crawl" is nothing short of a miracle. His favorite bit of his morning swim is to dive into the water on the back of his keeper.

# Blaze of Glory

Husband-and-wife team Cody and Sarah Rawson-Harris have made careers of training animals for movie and TV appearances, including teaching sheep to shake hands and horses to buck on cue. Even so, teaching stunt horses Abbey and Blowfly to jump through a wall of flames up to 20 feet high is impressive. The stunt took almost two months' training, starting with very small flames.

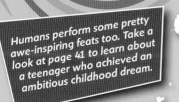

**ZOOM IN!**

Humans perform some pretty awe-inspiring feats too. Take a look at page 41 to learn about a teenager who achieved an ambitious childhood dream.

# ONE OF A KIND

## Pretty in Pink

Fishermen in Henan Province, China, discovered a real-life mutant turtle when they reeled in their nets. The three-legged, soft-shelled turtle was found in Poyang Lake, and its unusual color is thought to be a genetic mutation. The turtles, which are normally gray-brown, are a delicacy in Asia, where they are used in turtle soup and traditional medicine.

## Monkey Pig

This little piglet looks as if it might be more at home in the trees. The monkey-faced pig was one of a litter of five born in Henan Province, China. Its front legs are much shorter than its back legs, causing it to hop like a kangaroo. The piglet's appearance is thought to have been caused by a rare disorder that stops the eyes from separating normally.

# Strange Squid

This banded piglet squid is always smiling thanks to the skin pigments that give it a permanent grin. The deep-sea creature is the size of an orange when it fills its transparent body with water and its tentacles look like a wild mop of hair. It lives in almost total darkness more than 300 feet deep and has light-producing organs beneath its eyes.

## SAY WHAT!

A calf with three nostrils has become a local celebrity in Cheiry, Switzerland, where her fame has saved her from being sent to market with other calves.

# Seeing Double

Barbara and Frank Witte from California have five or six bearded dragon lizards, depending on whether you count Zak-n-Wheezie as one or two. The Wittes like to think of two-headed Zak-n-Wheezie as two lizards with one body and say that each has a distinct personality—Zak, on the right, is more boisterous, while Wheezie is more happy-go-lucky.

# ALL WASHED UP

## Shell Shiners

Green sea turtles line up to get a wash and brush-up at this yellow tang cleaning station. The tang feed on algae, which collects on the turtles' shells, so the fish get lunch while the turtles get clean and shiny shells.

## Open Wide

Hippopotamuses are known for being one of Africa's most dangerous large animals. They can kill with one snap of their powerful jaws, so this brave zebra was looking death in the face as it played dental hygienist and licked the hippo's razor-sharp teeth clean. The zebra was sharing an enclosure with the hippo and her baby at Zurich Zoo.

# Near Cat-Astrophe

Kimba, a Persian kitten from Sydney, Australia, survived a spin in a washing machine after climbing inside to curl up on the dirty laundry. Kimba's owner switched on the machine, which was luckily set to cold wash. Thirty minutes later he opened the door to hear a meow and the four-month-old kitten emerged shocked and bedraggled, but suffering nothing more than hypothermia and sore eyes.

## SAY WHAT!

Animal researchers in Japan have developed a CD of classical music with background noises such as dogs barking, human conversation, and crows crowing to help stressed-out dogs to relax.

# Canine Carwash

Lots of people get their cars cleaned when they visit the supermarket and now shoppers in Tokyo, Japan, can get their dogs washed, too. The automated pet-washing machine shampoos, rinses, and blow-dries a dog in 30 minutes, using eye-friendly soap, and water containing ozone for a fluffy, shining coat.

HELP!

# Index

**PHOTO CREDITS:** Ripley Entertainment Inc. and the editors of this book wish to thank the following photographers, agents and other individuals for permission to use and reprint the following photographs in this book. Any photographs included in this book that are not acknowledged below are property of the Ripley Archives. Great effort has been made to obtain permission from the owners of all material included in this book. Any errors that may have been made are unintentional and will gladly be corrected in future printings if notice is sent to Ripley Entertainment Inc., 7576 Kingspointe Parkway, Suite 188, Orlando, Florida 32819.

**COVER/TITLE PAGE:** Ripley Entertainment

**BACK COVER:** Dr. David Cox National Physical Laboratory UK; Image by Bryan Haeffele (www.bryanhaeffele.com) for Historic Hudson Valley (www.hudsonvalley.org); Granato Leandro.

**CONTENTS PAGE:** 2: Bizarre contact lenses—Kevin Smith/Solent News/Rex Features; Playing piano on fire—AP/Press Association Images; 2-3: Critter cruiser—www.firebox.com; 3: Turtle being washed by fish—Mike Roberts/Solent News/Rex Features; Yellowdog made of crayons—www.herbwilliamsart.com; Skyaking—Eli Thompson/Barcroft Media Ltd

**INTRO PAGES:** 4-5: Message paper—iStock.com; red tags—iStock.com; Grunge paper—iStock.com; 6: Mouse in stew—Quirky China News/Rex Features; Mickey Mouse dog—Robert N. Piercy; Guinness Rishi—Guinness Rishi; 7: Giant Turban—AFP/Getty Images

**CHAPTER 1: 10:** Crying face of an iceberg—Barcroft Media via Getty Images; Cave of crystals—Javier Trueba/MSF/Science Photo Library; **11:** Devil's Swimming Pool—Francisc Stugren; View of Africa's Victoria Falls—Photoshot/Imagebroker.net; **12:** Balanced rocks—Bill Dan/Rex Features; Giant sinkhole—Gobierno de Guatemala/ABACA/Press Association Images; **13:** New islands off Dubai: Reuters/Ho New; Spraying sand to create islands—Reuters/Anwar Mirza; The Kjeragbollten—Greg Epperson/www.photolibrary.com; **14:** Luminescent orchids—Reuters/Jonathan Drake; The legend of Milky Sea—Steve Haddock & Steve Miller; **15:** Colors in a bubble—© William Radcliffe/Science Faction/Corbis; Chinese flag made from flowers—© UPPA/Photoshot; **16:** Underground map tapestry—Andrew Hasson/Barcroft Media Ltd; Topsy turvy bus—Toby Talbot/AP/Press Association Images; **17:** Hotel in the shape of three Chinese gods—Wenn.com; Key card hotel room—Charles Sykes/Rex/Rex Features; **18:** Garage art—Anglia Press Agency Ltd/Rex Features; Tiny house—James Ambler/Barcroft USA; **19:** Bubble wrap street—Rex Features; Parking spaces picnic—Thibault Camus/AP/Press Association Images; **20-21:** Amazon walker—Photos by Keith Ducatel www.keithducatel.com; **22:** Only house standing—Photograph by Ray Asgar www.austinhehjet.com; Red river—Solent News/Rex Features; **23:** Sand storm—ChinaFotoPress/Photocome/Press Association Images; **24:** Mouse in stew—Quirky China News/Rex Features; Egg within egg—Sam Furlong/SWNS.com; **25:** Winning pumpkin—Scott Heckel/AP/Press Association Images; Fried bats—Getty Images; **27:** Globe—iStock.com; **28:** Polar dog mail—Steve Davey/Rex Features; Stamp art—David Burner/Rex Features; **29:** Card that grows flora—Getty Images; Smallest post service—Leafcutter Designs

**CHAPTER 2: 32:** The Portaledge—Greg Epperson/www.photolibrary.com; Wing suit—Getty Images; **33:** Professor Splash—Michael Martin/Barcroft Media Ltd; Underwater ice hockey—Wenn.com; **34:** Lava surfer—Kirk Lee Aeder/Barcroft Media Ltd; Skyaking—Eli Thompson/Barcroft Media Ltd; **35:** Acid lake adventurer—George Kourounis; **36:** Breaking blocks holding an egg—Joe Alexander; Massaging a lion—Matthew Tabaccos/Barcroft Media Ltd; **37:** Shaking hands with a squirrel—Alex Wood/SWNS.com; Inhaling a garden—Ben Landau/Brittany Veitch/Rex Features; **38-39:** Bull leaping—Barcroft Media Ltd; **40:** Visiting zoos—Barcroft Media Ltd; Dan Martin—Andy Weekes/Rex Features; **41:** Youngest girl to sail solo around the world—Daniel Munoz/Reuters; 13 year old climbs Mount Everest—Gopal Chitrakar/Reuters; **44:** Milk bottle art—Caters News Agency Ltd/Rex Features; Planting plants in potholes—Tim Stewart News/Rex Features; **45:** Spy tooth—SSPL via Getty Images; Butter in shoes—Photograph By Patrik Rosenberg/Scanpix, Camera Press London; **48:** Cutting hair upside down—Stringer Shanghai/Reuters; Dancing scuba divers—David Gray/Reuters; **49:** Levitating man—Charles Sykes/Rex Features; Giant turban—AFP/Getty Images; **50:** Chocolate wrestling—Reuters/Laszlo Balogh; Rocket festival—Jerome Favre/AP/Press Association Images; **51:** Indian color festival—AFP/Getty Images

**CHAPTER 3: 54:** Tongue helping soldier to see—Lewis Whyld/PA Wire/Press Association Images; Brain cooling helmet—Jullian Preston-Powers, ThermaHelm© Limited, www.thermahelm.com; **55:** Touchscreen arm—Chris Harrison, Densey Tan, Dan Morris - Microsoft Research & Carnegie Mellon University; **56:** Ghost radar—Junji Kurokawa/AP/Press Association Images; Face in clouds—Charles Wordsworth/SWNS.com; **57:** Ghost boy in demolition works—Hull News & Pictures; **58:** Dr. Peter Terren Telsa Coil—Peter Terren/Rex Features; The Thinker statue—© Justimagine - Fotolia.com; **59:** Dr. Peter Terren Telsa Coil—Peter Terren/Rex Features; **60:** Trees on Mars—NASA/JPL/University of Arizona; Buzz Lightyear in space—NASA/NASA/Rex Features; **61:** Moon dust watch—AFP/Getty Images; Sun in line with the road—Barcroft Pacific/Barcroft Media Ltd; **62:** Sliver molecules—iStock.com; **65:** Rubik's cube wonder—Rebecca Michael/Newspix/Rex Features; **66:** Heart surgery awake—CHI-Photo/Tom Parker/Rex Features; Sword swallower cowboy—Niall Carson/PA Archive/Press Association Images; **67:** Girl with backwards feet—Richard Drew/AP/Press Association Images; **68:** Snake detects seizures—KPA/Zuma/Rex Features; Flexible granny—David Caird/Newspix/Rex Features; **69:** Happy hat—Lauren McCarthy/Rex Features; Boy allergic to all foods—Matt Turner/Newspix/Rex Features; **70:** Home technology bus stop—Features North/Rex Features; Blood lamp—Chris Lobina/Rex Features; **71:** Sliding house—Rex Features; Baby bot—AFP/Getty Images; **72:** Robot wedding—Yuriko Nakao/Reuters; Shock absorbing material—Luke MacGregor/Reuters; **73:** Orange power wellies—Rex Features; Laptop jumper—Photograph By Joel Penn, Camera Press London

**CHAPTER 4: 76:** Jalisa Thompson—Ripley Entertainment; Lady with horn on her head—Quirky China News/Rex Features; **77:** Jyoti the smallest girl at school—Simon De Trey-White/Barcroft Media Ltd; **78:** Dog who swallowed pottery animals—Geoffrey Robinson/Rex Features; Fish stuck in fence—Eric Gay/AP/Press Association Images; **79:** Flowers that blossom once every 3,000 years—Quirky China News/Rex Features; Mobile chapel—Rex Features; **80:** Hanging heavy weights hooked in skin—Quirky China News/Rex Features; Biting through wire—Zhou Yan/Imaginechina; **81:** Elephant massage—© Barbara Walton/EPA/Corbis; Eating nettles—Geoffrey Swaine/Rex Features; **82-83:** Airfix plane—Plum Pictures; **84:** Underwater statues—Wilfredo Lee/AP/Press Association Images; Bright hearse—Solent News/Rex Features; **85:** BMW gravestone—Pete Lawson; Cardboard cut-out of dead husband—Caters News; **87:** Dragon watermelon—Takashi Itoh; **90:** Boy hanging from window by ears—Quirky China News/Rex Features; Drag car exploding—Chuck Robinson/AP/Press Association Images; **91:** Car through building—KPA/Zuma/Rex Features; **92:** Llama gold caddie—Getty Images; Longest tug-of-war—Jason Kimball; **93:** Teenager climbs wall of darts—Marcus Brandt/DPA/Press Association Images; Sliding pitch—AFP/Getty Images; **94:** School at 102—Quirky China News/Rex Features; Staple city—Peter Root/Rex Features; **95:** © Christoph Otto/Focus/Eyevine; Siamese apple—Isifa Image Service sro/Rex Features

**CHAPTER 5: 98:** Sneakers that turn into sandals—Solent News/Rex Features; Bizarre contact lenses—Kevin Smith/Solent News/Rex Features; **99:** Color-In Dress—Bournemouth News/Rex Features; Clothes art—NTI Media Ltd/Rex Features; **100:** Toilet roll art—Anastassia Elias/Solent News/Rex Features; Small figure in a walnut—ChinaFotoPress/Photocome/Press Association Images; **101:** Tiny trainset—Barcroft USA; Snowman less than one human hair wide—Dr. David Cox National Physical Laboratory UK; **102:** Balloon dragon—AFP/Getty Images; Giant Lego® Nintendo—Sean Kenney/Rex Features; **103:** Hand carved pumpkins—Image by Bryan Haeffele (www.bryanhaeffele.com) for Historic Hudson Valley (www.hudsonvalley.org); **104:** Petra Werle's creatures—Unimedia Images/Rex Features; Sentence on a wing—Europics; **105:** Magnus Muhr's dead fly art—Geoffrey Robinson/Rex Features; **106:** Boat in the shape of a guitar—Adam Ward/Newspix/Rex Features; Playing piano on fire—AP/Press Association Images; **107:** Tiny violin—Europics; Ice piano—Wenn.com; **108:** Eggbox art—Enno de Kroon, The Netherlands; Drawing with remote control car—Reuters/Suzanne Plunkett; **109:** Painting with eye—Granato Leandro; **110-111:** Bacteria art—Eshel Ben-Jacob; **112:** Face painting—James Kuhn/Rex Features; Guinness Rishi—Guinness Rishi; **113:** Star Wars tattoos—M & Y Agency Ltd/Rex Features; George Reiger Disney tattoos—Reuters/Tim Shaffer; **115:** Yellowdog made of crayons—www.herbwilliamsart.com; **116:** Weird cakes—Debbie does cakes/Debbie Goard/Rex Features; Dog chew sculptures—Nick Cunard/Rex Features; **117:** Jellybean art—Solent News & Photo Agency/Rex Features; Prize pumpkins—Scott Cummins

**CHAPTER 6: 120:** Mickey Mouse dog—Robert N. Piercy; Frog who swallowed a lightbulb—Caters News Agency Ltd/Rex Features; **121:** Marrow duck—SWNS.com; Albino alligator—© UPPA/Photoshot; **122:** Spectacled teals—© YNA/EPA/Corbis; Musical goldfish—Solent News/Rex Features; **123:** Greedy fish—Gavin Bernard/Barcroft Media Ltd; Troublesome elephant—Caters News; **124:** Fox cubs in grill—PPD/Rex Features; Cat in freezer—SWNS.com; **125:** Shark gives birth—Kelly Tarlton's Antarctic Encounter & Underwater World; **127:** Critter cruiser—www.firebox.com; **128:** Tiny lethal frog—Solent News/Rex Features; Mini horse—Jim Cole/AP/Press Association Images; **129:** Peanut the tiny pony—Photograph By Sam Barcroft © Barcroft Media Ltd; Tiny lamb—Jeremy Durkin/Rex Features; **130:** Happy face spider—Caters News; Close up of fleas—Steve Gschmeissner/Science Photo Library; **131:** Caterpillar leaf—Conny Sandland/Rex Features; Furry lobster—A FIFIS/AP/Press Association Images; **132-133:** Lion opening car door—www.sell-my-photo.co.uk; **134:** Rodeo monkey—Dan Callister/Rex Features; Orangutan swimming—Barcroft Media via Getty Images; **135:** Stunt horse—Newspix/Rex Features; **136:** Pink turtle—Wenn.com; Monkey-like piglet—Wenn.com; **137:** Piglet squid—Gary Florin/Rex Features; Two-headed dragon—Craig Kohlruss/Landov/Press Association Images; **138:** Turtle being washed by fish—Mike Roberts/Solent News/Rex Features; Hippo lets zebra clean teeth—Solent/Jill Stonsteby/Rex Features; **139:** Cat in washing machine—Annika Enderborg/Newspix/Rex Features; Dog in washing machine—Sinopix/Rex Features